CHAMPAGNE

Edible

Series Editor: Andrew F. Smith

EDIBLE is a revolutionary new series of books dedicated to food and drink that explores the rich history of cuisine. Each book reveals the global history and culture of one type of food or beverage.

Already published

Apple Erika Janik

Bread William Rubel

Cake Nicola Humble

Caviar Nichola Fletcher

Cheese Andrew Dalby

Chocolate Sarah Moss and Alexander Badenoch

Curry Colleen Taylor Sen

Dates Nawal Nasrallah

Hamburger Andrew F. Smith

Hot Dog Bruce Kraig

Ice Cream Laura B. Weiss

Lobster Elisabeth Townsend

Milk Hannah Velten

Olive Fabrizia Lanza

Pancake Ken Albala

Pie Janet Clarkson

Pizza Carol Helstosky

Potato Andrew F. Smith

Sandwich Bee Wilson

Soup Janet Clarkson

Spices Fred Czarra

Tea Helen Saberi

Whiskey Kevin R. Kosar

Champagne

A Global History

Becky Sue Epstein

REAKTION BOOKS

Published by Reaktion Books Ltd
33 Great Sutton Street
London EC1V 0DX, UK
www.reaktionbooks.co.uk

First published 2011

Copyright © Becky Sue Epstein 2011

Printed and bound in China by C&C Offset Printing Co. Ltd

British Library Cataloguing in Publication Data

Epstein, Becky Sue, 1952–
Champagne: a global history. – (Edible)
1. Champagne (Wine) 2. Champagne (Wine) – History.
I. Title II. Series
641.2 224-DC22

ISBN 978 1 86189 857 9

Contents

Bubbling Up to the Top: Champagne and Other Great Sparkling Wines

In the month of June, right in the middle of the recent recession, the world's longest champagne bar opened in London: 95.8 metres of confidence that travellers on the high-speed Eurostar train between London and Paris will continue to toast departures and arrivals in a celebratory manner – with a glass of champagne. Champagne bars like New York City's Flute and The Bubble Lounge are opening branches in San Francisco, London and Paris, while British department store Harvey Nichols recently launched a Belle Époque champagne bar at its flagship Knightsbridge store in London.

Champagne houses regularly sponsor film events, adding celebrity endorsements such as actress Scarlett Johansson's for Moët et Chandon at the 2009 Tokyo Film Festival. In the past few years, Veuve Clicquot has collaborated with car designer Porsche and boat designer Riva on champagne cabinets and carrying cases. Piper-Heidsieck, with several top fashion designers, created sexy accoutrements like Christian Louboutin's high-heeled glass slipper for sipping champagne, and Jean Paul Gaultier's red leather-bustier clad bottle. In 2008, Moët et Chandon commissioned designer Karl Lagerfeld to fashion a champagne glass for Dom Pérignon based on supermodel Claudia Schiffer's breast – an update of the shallow

Harvey Nichols' recently opened Fifth Floor Champagne Bar in London.

coupe glass supposedly designed in the shape of Marie Antoinette's breast. Often associated with actors and musicians, champagne makes news when a star endorses it – or disses it, as in 2006 when rapper and style-maker Jay-Z initiated a boycott of Louis Roederer's Cristal, which, until then, had been the champagne of choice for hip-hop artists and their fans.

Champagne continues to be the beverage that signals special occasions and celebrations, no matter what the climate or the economy is like – in life as well as on screen. In films, James Bond famously quaffed only the finest of everything. Bollinger is known as 007's signature champagne, though he occasionally sipped vintage Dom Pérignon. For a brief period Bond enjoyed Taittinger – imitating his creator, Ian Fleming – until a scene in 1963's *From Russia With Love* when poison was slipped into Tatiana Romanova's glass, at which point 007's relationship with that champagne also expired.

Originally drunk only by the wealthy nobility, champagne and other sparkling wines have now infiltrated much of the

Claudia Schiffer-inspired champagne glass, created by Karl Lagerfeld for
Dom Pérignon.

The first champagne-only bar in Paris, at Le Dokhan's Hotel, carries over 50 champagnes.

wine-drinking population and are automatically included in life's milestones; seemingly, there can't be a wedding or anniversary celebration without them. Every sporting triumph requires jets of fizz to celebrate. New ships are christened with champagne before their maiden voyages, and it is joyously presented at the end of hot-air balloon rides. People around the globe cannot contemplate New Year's Eve without plenty of bubbles.

Modern rulers have sustained the tradition of celebrating with sparkling wine – if not always with champagne. us president Barack Obama had 100 bottles of Italian sparkling wine served at a dinner on his inaugural weekend in 2009, while an American sparkler was on the menu for the luncheon following his inauguration ceremony.

Sparkling wines are highly valued all over the world. Why are these wines called 'sparkling wines'? Because, though champagne is a sparkling wine, it is only one of many sparkling wines made in wine regions throughout the world. Champagne is the name for quality sparkling wines produced in the region of Champagne, about 100 miles east of Paris. Champagne is unquestionably the most famous sparkling wine. From the 1700s on, Champagne's producers have essentially branded the category of sparkling wine as their own. Champagne is so highly regarded that we tend to refer to all sparkling wines as 'champagnes' even when they do not come from Champagne.

In theory, any sparkling wine can be as good or better than any champagne – though the Champagne producers have been at it for so long that many of their sparkling wines are not only much more famous than sparkling wines from other regions, but are also excellent wines. To enhance their own identities, some quality sparkling wines from other countries have proprietary names. For instance, the sparkling wine originating in Catalonia, Spain, is called cava; northern Italy has prosecco and asti (among others); while sekt is a popular sparkler in Germany and Austria. In all these regions the

Map of the Champagne region in France.

sparkling wines are made primarily with regionally native grapes. Though sparkling beverages can be made from many things, this book limits the discussion to wines made with traditional wine grapes (*Vitis vinifera*), not table grapes or other fruits. In Champagne, the sparkling wines are made mainly with white chardonnay and red pinot noir grapes, with smaller amounts of another red grape, pinot meunier, often blended in.

In the US and other New World wine regions, sparkling wines can be made with any grapes. (New World refers to wine regions other than Europe.) Lacking their own proprietary names, these non-champagne sparklers are simply referred to as 'sparkling wines' – a generic term for an effervescent wine without referencing a particular quality level or geographic designation. Erroneously, it is often assumed that without a designated name like champagne or cava, a sparkling wine is nothing to be proud of, but that is far from the truth.

Why is champagne perceived by so many people to be *the* top-quality sparkling wine? The short answer is that to date, the most expensive and highest ranked sparkling wines in the world have come from Champagne. And the people of Champagne have been publicizing this for hundreds of years.

So why doesn't everyone simply call their sparkling wine champagne? If so many consumers are confused, why don't sparkling wine producers take advantage of this and align their products with the most well-known sparkling wines of quality? Unfortunately, some of them do. But the best producers who are not located in the Champagne region do not use the word 'champagne' on their labels. For over a hundred years French champagne producers have fought to maintain their own proprietary name, to keep it geographically delimited and quality controlled. The European Union (EU) now

Over the past three centuries champagne has been served in a variety of glasses, from flat coupes to tall, narrow flutes, and many shapes in between.

supports this, and non-EU nations are also signing an agreement with champagne producers not to use the term outside of Champagne.

Sekt, cava and crémant are all familiar terms in EU nations, and are becoming more well known in the US, the UK and the rest of the world. However, the UK and the US have not yet chosen proprietary names for their sparkling wines, which arguably does not help the worldwide perception of their products.

Champagne first became famous as a somewhat sweet wine in the late 1600s, and demand for it increased steadily throughout the eighteenth century. During the 1800s, when winemaking techniques improved and fashion demanded it, the winemakers produced half-dry (demi-sec) champagne. Later they were able to produce first the 'extra dry' style and finally the very dry brut, which became overwhelmingly popular in the 1900s. Today, the most widely known style of sparkling wine in the Western world is brut. Currently, there is a new trend toward an even 'drier' or more 'natural' style

Rosé champagne can range in colour from pale pink or peach to deep rose or salmon. Here are a few of the hues.

of champagne called nature or brut nature (also referred to as zéro dosage).

Champagnes and sparkling wines come in many colours, shading from pale straw through yellow into gold. Rosé sparkling wines have recently become extremely fashionable, and are growing more popular every year. Rosé sparkling wines range from light orange and pale pink into apricot, salmon, rose-pink and even clear, light red – depending on the style of production and which grapes are used. Most rosé champagnes are now made in the brut style.

Sparkling wine consumption and spending have been trending up on every continent – while mirroring dips in the economy. Escalation is most noticeable in the areas of the world where cultural Westernization has risen the most dramatically, though the trend reflects luxury fads as well as the increased availability of lower-priced sparkling wines. From

2002 to 2008, Russia's spending on sparkling wines went up over 200 per cent while India's and China's increases weren't far behind. In countries such as Brazil and Ireland, spending increased by almost 300 per cent. Even France and the UK were up around 65 per cent. Australians spent about 120 per cent more, though US spending increased only around 20 per cent, with South Africa and Canada in between, at around 75 per cent.

Sparkling wines have been stylish for over 300 years, and demand is likely to continue increasing with the globalization of food and wine culture. Champagnes and sparkling wines are no longer reserved for important occasions; people are popping open the fizz for just about any type of festivity, small or large, even a simple dinner party.

I

The Origins of Champagne

By the Middle Ages, Champagne's wines were well known in certain areas of France. But because Champagne's vineyards were so far north, it was difficult to ripen the grapes before autumn's rains and cool temperatures. The finished wines were light red and somewhat acidic – which did, however, enable them to last longer in the barrel without spoiling. Wine producers along the Marne river in Champagne began shipping their wines to buyers in Paris as well as London and Flanders, attempting to compete with the wines of Burgundy. At that time, all wines were still wines ('still' is the term for wine that does not have bubbles in it); fizz was considered undesirable.

So how did Champagne become the most famous region in the world for making sparkling wines? In fact, Champagne was not the first place where sparkling wine is known to have been popular. As early as 1516, sparkling wines were produced in the Languedoc region of southern France. The first trade in them was recorded in 1531 at the Benedictine abbey of St Hilaire in a village in the foothills of Limoux – a cool, mountainous, winemaking area near the Mediterranean. This was over 100 years before the birth of Dom Pérignon, the man generally considered to be the originator of champagne.

Parchment record of sparkling wine trade in 1544 in Limoux, in the south of France – over 100 years before Dom Pérignon went to Champagne.

In fact, the production method for the wine Blanquette de Limoux is the same as that used for the first sparkling wines in Champagne in the late seventeenth century. After the grapes were pressed, naturally occurring yeasts began fermenting the grape juice – converting the sugars to alcohol – until winter's cold caused fermentation activity to die down. At that point, unbeknownst to the winemakers, the yeasts were merely dormant. In Limoux, the wine was bottled during the first full moon in March. Afterwards, as the weather warmed, the yeasts became active again, and fermentation started up within the sealed bottles. Bubbles developed because carbon dioxide (CO_2) was also a by-product of the fermentation process. The bubbles were trapped in the liquid in the bottles, creating carbonated or 'sparkling' wine. All sparkling wine was originally produced – or occurred – in this way.

Copy of a 16th-century tapestry showing an idealized version of the grape harvest in Champagne.

Limoux was too far from Paris to influence Parisians' drinking habits. However, it is clear that the phenomenon of carbonated or sparkling beverages was engaging a variety of people in the 1600s. One, the Englishman Christopher Merret, presented a paper to the Royal Society in 1662 that dicussed sparkling apple cider along with its bottling and secondary fermentation. This occurred six years before the monk Dom Pérignon arrived at the Hautvillers monastery where he is popularly thought to have 'invented' champagne.

Though Champagne is barely a couple of hours' drive north-east of Paris today, a few hundred years ago it was several days' journey from the French capital. Outside of big cities, most people never went beyond their local market town for food or wine. Around the towns of Reims, Épernay and Troyes – merchant centres of the Champagne district – people drank their local red and white wines, but several of the towns in the region were located along major rivers, making

An illustration of the annual grape harvest and winemaking in the countryside in the early 16th century. Nicolas Le Rouge, *Le Grand Calendrier et Compost des Bergers*, 1529.

it easier for barrels of Champagne's wines to be exported to Paris, and beyond.

These barrels of wine were commonly purchased by tavern owners, sometimes by wealthy aristocrats. They hoped to use as much wine as possible as soon as each barrel was breached because they knew that wine in opened barrels deteriorated, especially in warmer weather. Once a cask was opened they would transfer the wine to jugs or bottles, mainly as needed for serving. In France in the 1600s, bottles were hand-blown, fairly fragile and somewhat irregular in shape so they could not be stoppered effectively. In barrel or bottle, the wine would not maintain its quality for long.

Meanwhile, there were reports from England that when tavern-keepers opened barrels of wine from Champagne in the spring, sometimes the wine was fizzy – and some of the Englishmen liked it! Fizzy wine soon became so fashionable that people began experimenting with methods to make wine bubbly. Tavern owners had already been adding sugar both for flavouring and to counteract the acidity of Champagne's wines. They found that adding sugar sometimes made the wine more effervescent – for the same reason Blanquette de Limoux sparkled in the south of France, though they would not have been aware of this. When new wines were put in barrels and shipped out of Champagne it was late autumn, and cold. The fermentation process had stopped – or so they thought. With warmer weather, the yeasts began functioning again, rapidly consuming the grape sugars that were left in the wine. Some of the resultant carbon dioxide remained in the barrel-enclosed wine, making it fizzy.

But still wine was the goal in Champagne, when Dom Pierre Pérignon arrived to become treasurer of the Benedictine Abbey of Hautvillers in 1668, when he was twenty-nine years old. (Dom is a monk's title at Benedictine and other monasteries.) Traditionally, monks had produced much of the wine in Europe, and funded many monasteries with proceeds from wine sales. The monks were aware there was a demand for a new, finer style of wine at this point in history. Dom Pérignon decided to become involved in every aspect of the winemaking process so he rolled up his sleeves and began at ground level, so to speak, in the vineyards and the winery. Dom Pérignon insisted on rigorous pruning in the vineyard, resulting in higher quality, optimally flavoured grapes. In the winery, he laboured for years to produce consistently excellent wines. First he worked to create clear, fine-flavoured, still wines. But around 1700, sparkling wines had become too fashionable to ignore. So he began developing new practices for the vineyard and winery, which soon became the acknowledged standards. He used lightly pressed pinot noir grapes for his champagne. In an extremely delicate pressing, the white interiors of the grapes were squeezed out

A current view of Hautvillers, Dom Pérignon's monastery. The abbey was founded around AD 650, and served as a monastery until 1791.

Early champagne grape press, similar to those used in the 17th century.

and pressed, while ideally the black skins of the pinot noir grapes remained behind. In the late seventeenth century, there would have been some (red) grape skins in the juice, making the wine light red, not clear white. Dom Pérignon thought white grapes made a wine too sour and unpredictable to use in his sparkling wines.

Cork stoppers had been known to the French and English in Roman times, over 1,000 years before. It is as much a mystery why this knowledge had been lost in France, as why it was regained by the French at this particular moment. Speculation has it that travelling Iberian monks brought cork to France, and Dom Pérignon seized upon this to stopper his effervescent wine.

Because of the pressure in the bottle, Dom Pérignon began tying the corks onto the bottlenecks with lengths of twine. He thought too much time in barrels made the wine dull, so he began experimenting with bottles. But the bottles kept exploding because the bubbly champagne exerted pressure on the delicate French glass. Any bottle could shatter if bumped, or a flaw in the glass could cause it to explode. Not only did this endanger the workers, it also made the wine difficult to transport, and ultimately very expensive because so much champagne was lost.

When the same wine was transported by barrel to England and bottled there, these explosions rarely occurred. The English had rediscovered cork stoppers for bottles, perhaps as early as Shakespeare's time. More importantly, in the seventeenth century English glass was manufactured using coal instead of wood fires, and this made glass considerably stronger. English wine merchants were using glass bottles made this way by 1630, nearly a century before the process became common in France.

When Dom Pérignon succeeded in producing great champagne in a bottle, perhaps, as legend has it, he did call out: 'Brothers, I am drinking stars!' It's a wonderful fable,

Dom Pérignon, the fabled monk who is said to have 'invented' champagne, from a sculpted relief at his Hautvillers Abbey.

Champagne's famously chalky soil.

one that the current mega champagne producer Moët et Chandon has been careful to nurture, especially as the firm's top champagne is named Dom Pérignon. There is a statue of the famous monk in front of the Moët et Chandon headquarters in Epernay.

Dom Pérignon died in 1715 at the age of seventy-six. Within a few years of his death, his vineyard management and winemaking techniques had become the prime references for champagne producers. They learned to make sure that the vines did not grow rampantly, putting too much energy into stems and leaves at the expense of the grapes. Records kept at Hautvillers assisted vine growers and wine producers for centuries.

Another monk from this abbey, Dom Ruinart, made an important contribution to champagne production. He began storing the bottles of champagne in chalk quarries that the Romans had dug under the city of Reims. Underground, the temperature remained between 50 and 60°F (10–14°C) year round and the chalky soil was also relatively easy to carve when more wine storage space was needed. Fortunately, around this time the French also learned the secret of producing the stronger glass bottles necessary to contain frothy champagne. Dom Ruinart's nephew Nicolas was one of the first traders – and producers – active in the newly created sparkling wine trade, founding Champagne Ruinart, the oldest champagne firm in the world, in 1729.

2
The Cult and Culture
of Champagne

The tradition of celebrating with champagne began with French royalty, who had enjoyed the wines of Champagne since the end of the fifth century AD when their reigning monarch, Clovis, was baptized in the cathedral at Reims. It became a tradition for the kings of France to be crowned in Reims Cathedral, and to mark the celebration with the wines of Champagne.

As far back as the eleventh century, the wines of Aÿ in the Champagne region were well known outside the region because Pope Urban II came from this area. King François I had prized these wines in the early sixteenth century, as did Henry III later in the century, when one of his trusted advisors married into the Sillery family from the area near Reims. The advisor's wife brought her family's wine to the court, and from then on Sillery wine was in demand. Though now rarely recognized outside of Champagne, Sillery was one of the first significant champagnes.

Eighteenth-century winemakers in Champagne learned to stabilize the production of their sparkling wine, enabling them to create and service markets in countries as distant as the US and Russia. Many of today's most famous champagne houses originated during the eighteenth century; in addition

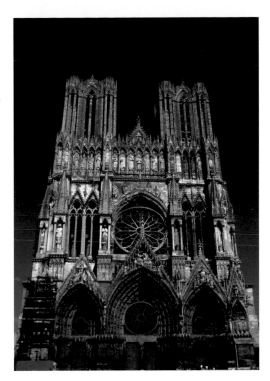

The cathedral at Reims, built originally in the early 13th century, is the site of the coronations of many generations of French kings.

to Ruinart, there were pioneers like Moët, Piper-Heidsieck and Gosset, whose champagnes are among the best known even today.

Through the 1700s and early 1800s, the evolving business was impeded by sporadic climatic and economic factors including periodic poor grape harvests and wars that encompassed France and Champagne's export destinations. But the merchants of Champagne were aided by political events as well. Early in the eighteenth century, the champagne business was really set in motion by new transportation policies. In its native land, champagne's popularity was expanding. As in other countries, royal courts in France during most of the

A village in the Champagne region, in autumn, looking much as it has done for hundreds of years.

eighteenth century were legendary for their excesses. The ruling regent of France from 1715 to 1723 was the powerful Philippe II, Duc d'Orleans, who apparently spent much of his time under the influence of champagne. An often quoted 1716 letter from the duke's mother contains a claim that her son drank only the wines of Champagne, which were basically wholesome, being so gentle and frothy.

With a few sips – or more likely a few glasses – everyone became wittier, more attractive and much less restrained. Philippe's handsome nephew, King Louis XV, subscribed to this theory when he took the throne in 1723. This affinity no doubt contributed to the champagne producers having the king's ear. In 1728, the champagne industry was changed by a royal decree allowing the wines of Champagne – and only Champagne – to be transported in bottles. (All other wines had to be shipped in barrels.) This momentous ruling meant that finished, bottled sparkling wine could be sent directly to consumers not only in France, but to England, Holland and other countries.

A variety of merchants, honest and otherwise, attempted to produce and distribute champagne. Some of them became producers, like pioneer Nicolas Ruinart, who had been in the wool business. Ruinart didn't have his own vineyards, but he and his father began to bottle and age champagne. He began selling champagne to his existing wool customers. In 1730, he sold only 130 bottles, but the champagne business grew so rapidly that by 1739, Ruinart had just about given up his wool trade to deal in wine. Nicolas's son Claude was even more of a marketer, and became a man of influence in Reims.

Some brokers began to make the champagne themselves, like Claude Moët, who grew grapes in Champagne. Though the firm Moët et Chandon dates its establishment from 1743, Moët himself had been a wine trader since the early

Basket of harvested grapes in Champagne.

part of the century when he began to travel to the royal palace at Versailles to sell his wines in person. He was able to gain audiences with influential people not only because of his strong salesmanship, but also because of his own pedigree: an ancestor of his had fought with Joan of Arc in the fifteenth century.

In 1735, Louis xv publicly took an additional interest in this favourite royal beverage, and declared the amount, type of bottle and closure to be used for the sparkling wines of Champagne: there should be no less than 25 ounces in a bottle, with three strings to be used in tying on the cork. The bottle (*flacon*) was bulb-shaped with a long, narrow neck. Sometimes the coat of arms of the producer was imprinted on the glass. Champagne was gaining its own identity in the wine world.

Now it was up to the merchants of Champagne to open up new markets. Many were already dealing in cloth, wool, thread and other associated goods with customers in neighbouring countries and provinces, and trading with large cities from Paris to the Low Countries and the British Empire. Soon after quantities of champagne were ordered by the tastemakers in Paris and Versailles, demand for this new, sparkling beverage multiplied further.

By the mid-1700s, Claude Moët was supplying champagne to Louis xv's mistress, Madame de Pompadour, and producing more champagne than the entire rest of the region. Champagne was being served at all important events in the court. As early as 1735, the king had commissioned several paintings of an idealized champagne lifestyle by well-known artists of the era: *Le Déjeuner d'Huitres* by Jean-François de Troy and *Le Déjeuner au Jambon* by Nicolas Lancret.

Once Moët got his contract to supply the court at Versailles, he was still taking great chances because champagne producers commonly lost 20 per cent or more of their bottles during production, storage and transportation – and sometimes as much as 90 per cent. Somehow, Moët kept his losses low. By 1762 he was the largest champagne producer in the region, also exporting champagne to clients in England, Frankfurt, Madrid and Russia.

Ragingly popular at the French court, champagne's influence swelled rapidly. Monarchs of the time were absolute and terrifying in their power. If they – and their wives, influential courtiers and mistresses – wanted to drink champagne, everyone raised their glasses and drank champagne. Champagne became the most sought-after libation of celebration for the elite in the capitals of the Western world as the eighteenth century moved forward. In Russia, Peter the Great began the tradition of drinking champagne at his court, which he handed down to his daughter Elizabeth. Later, the insatiable Catherine the Great who ruled Russia during the second half of the eighteenth century was a fervent believer in the aphrodisiac powers of champagne.

At times, champagne was a victim of politics and wars outside of France. It was difficult to export champagne during the Polish wars of succession (1733–8) and the Austrian wars of succession (1741–8). Late in the century, 1776 was both a bad and a good year in champagne commerce. It was the beginning of the US war of independence, with the British blockade of American ports. In Champagne, producers experienced the highest breakage of bottles ever, which was blamed on particularly explosive yeasts. But during the same year, champagne commerce was deregulated and it was no longer under royal supervision. Now, anyone who desired could enter the field and try their hand at brokering champagne.

After the French Revolution the monasteries were disbanded, and, with demand skyrocketing, anyone who could get their hands on grapes or wines was making champagne. George Washington, the first president of the anti-monarchist United States, served champagne at a state dinner in 1796: champagne consumption was no longer just for the titled aristocracy.

Champagne's merchants were now generally the same brokers who bottled and aged the sparkling wines. They bought grapes or wine on credit from grape growers who thought of themselves as farmers (or simple, base winemakers) not entrepreneurs. Merchants took on the great risks of bottling the wine, storing and shipping it while absorbing the costs of breakage, finding buyers and creating new markets. Often the merchants delayed paying the growers and winemakers. Some increased the winemakers' dependence on them by supplying their wine barrels, too. Often, the merchants paid the grape growers last, and the poor farmers could do nothing about this. (Because of this system, which survives today, there is still some antagonism between growers and champagne houses.)

Champagne producers held all the power in pricing as well: they were the only ones who knew the true amount of champagne stores hidden in their deep cellars. This was the situation at the end of the eighteenth century, when France was in a state of political upheaval. Champagne producers still sold to their elite, aristocratic markets, but with ruling power shifting every few years, the producers also sought other markets outside of France.

Most of the original champagne-company owners were men with family businesses. They spent considerable time on the road, crisscrossing the continent, travelling to or hiring brokers as far away as England, Russia and America, building awareness of champagne and making sales to a broader base of customers including those at the top of the newly rising bourgeois class. The haute bourgeoisie aspired to be like the class above them. This commercially successful group dressed sumptuously and built great houses where they ate and drank ostentatiously: a perfect target for the travelling marketers of champagne. Champagne became the first table wine to be shipped all over the world.

3
Champagne is Established

From the mid-1700s through the 1800s, champagne evolved from a small merchant enterprise into an industry, aided by advances in chemistry, biology and mechanization, and a consistent awareness of the importance of marketing. There were quite a few new players willing to gamble on this new trade before 1800. In addition to Ruinart and Gosset, early champagne houses that are well known today include Moët et Chandon, founded in 1743; Henri Abelé, 1757; Lanson and Delamotte, 1760; Veuve Clicquot, 1772; Roederer, 1776; and Piper-Heidsieck, 1785. The producers began to use grapes from the same vineyards year after year, recognizing that the soil and aspect of the vineyards – as well as the grower's skill – were reflected in the consistency and quality of the grapes.

What was it like to drink the sparkling wine of Champagne in its early days? There are no very old bottles of champagne we can uncork and enjoy today – except in the occasional re-discovered shipwreck. Though some champagnes do last for decades, they aren't made to last for centuries, and certainly not as sparkling wines; they would definitely lose their bubbles. But we do know how champagne was made centuries ago, and what it was like.

A typical view in the Champagne region, unchanged for centuries (except for pavements and electrical wires). This shows the castle of Boursault, not far from the Marne river.

An early style of champagne glass that was fashionable from the late 17th century to about 1755.

As with all eighteenth- and nineteenth-century wines, champagne tasted slightly sweet. In fact a little sweetness is very desirable for pairing with food; slightly sweet wines (also known as 'off-dry' wines) tend to complement many dishes. The colour of Champagne's early sparkling wine was usually light red – a salmon, pink or rose hue – because red -grapes were lightly pressed to make champagne, adding only a little of the colour from the grape skins to the wine.

In terms of bubbles, champagnes varied. The French referred to champagnes as *pétillant, demi-mousseux, mousseux* and *grand mousseux* (roughly translated as lightly sparkling, half-sparkling, sparkling and super-sparkling). The amount of fizz depended on bottle pressure. The highest bottle pressure early technology could achieve was three atmospheres (roughly half of today's champagnes).

Champagne was originally served in a cone-shaped glass like a flute with straight sides, directly connected to its glass base (or foot), and without a stem. It wasn't until the late eighteenth century that the coupe – the wide, shallow, stemmed glass – gained popularity. The coupe is supposedly based on the shape of the breast of a noblewoman of the French court, anyone from Madame de Pompadour to Marie Antoinette, depending on which story you prefer. The coupe would become the most popular champagne glass through the nineteenth century and most of the twentieth century.

Marketing to the upper classes was as important a century or two ago as it is now, in order to protect and maintain champagne's worldwide reputation. A key figure who succeeded in this endeavour was a woman whose name has become synonymous with fine champagne: Veuve Clicquot. The widow (*veuve*) Clicquot has long been celebrated in the world of champagne; she is known as the first great marketer of champagne wines. Today, her name graces some of the

Shelves full of handwritten records at the champagne house Veuve Clicquot date back to 1772.

best-known champagnes in the world, which are still produced by the company she helped establish with her husband at the end of the eighteenth century. Her young husband François died suddenly in 1805, when he was thirty-one years old. The new widow was then in her late twenties. With wealth on both her family's and her husband's side, she probably did not need to make money. Initially she and her father-in-law planned to dissolve the company. But she was from a hard-working merchant family, and decided instead to take on the company's management herself.

Her first years were tough, with Napoleon's war against the British on one side, and on the other front, war with Russia. In 1806, the Clicquot company lost almost one-third of its annual production in a British blockade of French ports. When the blockade was extended to the Baltic with Russia's declaration of war on Sweden in 1808, it was impossible to get goods through. Without their commercial profits, few nobles were buying champagne, and Clicquot drifted almost to a halt. In 1810 the widow relaunched the business under her own name, Veuve Clicquot-Ponsardin. Still, there was no profit in the champagne business for several years. In 1814, war was on her doorstep: the Cossacks, Prussians and Russians captured Reims on their way to Paris. Veuve Clicquot frantically walled up her champagne in the cellars, hoping the newly made partitions would escape detection by enemy soldiers. (Walling up cellars in Champagne would be repeated many times in the next 130 years, through the twentieth century's two world wars.)

Many of Champagne's cellars were ransacked by invading armies. But when peace came in 1814, the enemy officers took something important home with them: a taste for the sparkling wines of Champagne. Three years earlier, Champagne had experienced a wonderful harvest which people thought was caused by a large comet streaking across the night skies. Veuve Clicquot sent this lucky 'Vin de la Comète' to Russia in 1814. She took a big gamble sending the wines before the truce was signed, betting that her wines would get to a country deprived of champagne for years, just when they needed it to celebrate peace. Her luck held, and she cornered the Russian market. Veuve Clicquot made sure that a substantial part of it remained hers by commanding ship captains that carried her champagne not to make other stops on the way to Russia, and not to carry any other champagnes. Clicquot's exports to Russia increased dramatically, and this profitable state of affairs continued for decades.

Soon, more champagne producers began to trade with Russia; French champagne was the libation of choice for the Russian court. The sweetness of the champagne of that period captured the Russian taste; Russian royals had several special sweet blends (*cuvées*) created for them throughout the nineteenth century. The most famous is Cristal, which dates from 1876 and was made for the tsars by the champagne house of Roederer, which also supplied an important share of the Russian market. At that time Roederer was 100 years old, and it continued as 'Official Supplier to the Imperial Court of Russia' until the Russian Revolution forty years later. The Russians continued to favour sweet wines through the twentieth century, often toasting with them after dinner.

By contrast, the English had access to port wine for sipping at the end of the meal, due to well-established trade with Portugal that had begun during a war with France in the seventeenth century. The British aristocracy began to take their champagne at the beginning of the meal, and they started asking the champagne producers to make it drier. However, more than eighty years would elapse before truly dry champagne was possible.

In the mean time, the French sought a greater understanding of champagne production in order to create a consistent product. Enter the Napoleonic era's great – if little known – contributions to the world of wine. The first was by chemist Jean-Antoine Chaptal, who served as Napoleon's Home Secretary for the first five years of the nineteenth century. Chaptal understood the process of winemaking, and advocated adding some sugar to the just-pressed wine in Champagne. Adding a little sugar to Champagne's wines gave the yeasts more to work on: the result was a few per cent more alcohol in the finished product. To this day, the process of *chaptalization* (named after Chaptal) is a legal component of wine production in some regions of France, including Champagne.

In 1836, a local pharmacist named André François determined how much sugar should be present in a bottle of finished champagne. Too much sugar, and the yeasts would create too much CO_2. Too much carbonated pressure and the champagne bottles would burst. Regulating this didn't alleviate all the problems of bottle breakage immediately, but it helped the producers create much more consistent products in terms of taste as well as bubbles.

A bottle-filling machine had been invented in 1825, and a machine was invented to put corks into bottles in 1827. A good number of the 'Grandes Marques' (great champagne houses) were established early in the nineteenth century, and they were ready to apply this new knowledge. Henriot was founded in 1808; Perrier-Jouët in 1811; Laurent-Perrier in 1812; Billecart-Salmon in 1818; G. H. Mumm and Bollinger in the late 1820s. More great champagne houses appeared in the 1830s, including Boizel, Deutz and Pommery.

By 1840, production of champagne was well on its way to standardization – though there were still some undiscovered processes that would make a significant difference in production methods later in the century. At this time, the grapes were harvested, immediately pressed, then fermented into wine. Sugar was added, the wine was put into sealed bottles and the tops were tied on for the secondary fermentation to take place in the bottle. As always, many bottles cracked or exploded during this fermentation, the broken containers cascading rivers of champagne through the cellars, and sometimes injuring or even killing cellar workers.

After the second fermentation was completed (when the yeasts died), the bottles, which had been stored horizontally, were placed in a special wooden rack with angled slots called a *pupitre*. Bottles were hand-shifted a quarter turn each day, and given a little shake at the same time. The bottoms of the bottles were also gradually lifted so the tops pointed downward at an increasing angle. Gradually, the dead yeast cells and any other organic matter slid into the neck of the bottle. This process, called *remuage*, was invented in Veuve Clicquot's cellars in the second decade of the nineteenth century.

Each batch of wine was then analysed: a *gleuco-œnomètre* to measure sugar content had been invented by Cadet de Vaux in 1823. With the chemist François's formula, the proper dosage was concocted – 'dosage' was basically sugar dissolved into wine or spirits. (Other flavouring experiments were tried, but wine and sugar eventually became standard.)

Then came another dangerous procedure: opening the fizzy bottles to add the dosage. When the bottle caps were loosened, the plugs of organic matter spewed out with some of the bubbling wine, and the dosage was quickly added in its place to create the desired flavours and sweetness of the wine, as well as simply to re-fill the bottles to the correct levels. Workers often wore iron masks, but even this was not enough. The bottle caps shot off with great force, sometimes through slits in the masks and into a worker's eyes, blinding him for life. The final corks were hastily inserted and tied down – initially with string and later with a wire capsule called a *muselet*, developed in 1844 by Adolphe Jacquesson, of the well-known Jacquesson champagne house.

Additional industrial advancement between 1844 and 1846 included machines for rinsing bottles, for securing corks and for adding the dosage. Champagne producers mechanized gradually, as they could afford – or chose to afford – improvements. Many cellars remained extremely dangerous places to work for decades after the latest inventions, either because the new machines weren't installed right away, or because the machines didn't always work as promised.

While these new inventions were being adopted, champagne continued to soar in popularity. It was inevitable that winemakers in neighbouring regions would try their hands at sparkling wine – which they did as early as the 1820s in Burgundy. This was the beginning of a worldwide war the champagne producers have been waging ever since to protect their unique status by preventing other regions from using the alluring name 'champagne'.

Champagne houses became known for their proprietary styles. Each would blend wines from many vineyards to produce wines with identifiably similar aromas, flavours and even bubbles, year after year. They had the means to store some of their still wines while waiting to blend them with other vintages. This was in marked contrast to the rest of the wine world, where wines varied significantly from vintage to vintage. Part of a champagne's character also came from the house's long-term contracts with grape growers – most of the best from inside what later became the official boundaries of the champagne-growing region.

New methods of transportation, like the railway that came to the Champagne region in the mid-1800s, made possible significant strides in champagne's expansion during the rest of the century. If only nature would comply. The first vineyard plague, oidium (powdery mildew) arrived in 1852. Downy mildew was the second, in 1878. Neither of these diseases could be eradicated, but it was discovered that the vines could be dusted with sulphur and a copper sulphate mixture for an effective treatment when necessary.

In between these plagues of nature came a human outbreak: the Franco-Prussian war, in 1870. This was another devastating blow to the exporters of champagne as the US wine market was just recovering from the country's Civil War (1861–65). The original 'Champagne Charlie', Charles Heidsieck, had triumphantly toured the US, beginning in Boston in 1852 and thrilling people with his wit and charm – but the Civil War put an end to champagne imports.

This was also the time of the ascendancy of the second of Champagne's three famously innovative widows: Louise Pommery. After her husband died in 1858 when she was thirty-nine, she took over his red wine business, Pommery & Greno, and turned it into an extremely prosperous champagne house. Just before the start of the Franco-Prussian War, the energetic widow Pommery had begun experimenting with making a dry champagne. Word had come from London and New York that many people were tiring of sweet champagne (unlike in Russia and Eastern Europe). After the war she resumed her experimentation, and in 1874 – which also happened to be one of the top vintages of the century – Pommery succeeded in creating brut champagne.

In the region of Champagne, as the nineteenth century progressed, more and more champagne houses were established. Among them were Krug and Pol Roger in the 1840s, J. Lemoine and Duval-Leroy in the 1850s, Ayala, Canard-Duchêne and Alfred Gratien in the 1860s; in mid-century

The buildings of Champagne Ayala, photographed in 1910, before a major grape-growers' riot. They destroyed the champagne house in 1911; it was rebuilt the following year.

Philipponnat 'modernized' to sell champagne, though the family had been growing grapes and trading wine since at least 1522. Some vineyard owners became producers, but in general only businessmen – merchants, traders, bankers – and aristocrats had access to the capital necessary to establish a new wine company. Champagne Ayala, for instance, was founded by Edmond de Ayala, a Colombian diplomat descended from an aristocratic Spanish family. Part of his French wife's dowry consisted of vineyards in Champagne's Mareuil and Mareuil-sur-Aÿ.

More and more vineyard owners and small winemakers committed to growing grapes and making (still) wines to supply the champagne houses. At the beginning of the nineteenth century champagne producers were selling 600,000 bottles annually; at the end of the century they were selling 30 million bottles. From labels on bottles to posters, postcards and other advertising, champagne placed itself in the mind of the public as a top-class beverage. Towards the end of the nineteenth century champagne was regularly served at nightclubs from the legendary Maxim's to those frequented by the new middle class. Champagne was an aspiration for the nouveaux riches, merchants and other moderately wealthy people who were not aristocratic by birth. It was the symbol of glamour.

Champagne was also emblematic of flying, from the early days of manned balloon rides, which began in France in 1783. Hot-air balloons were as erratic in their ascent as they were in descent, and often landed their pilots miles away, in the midst of farmland. Terrified and threatened by the magical beings from the sky, farmers would run out to defend their fields. Purportedly, the balloon pilots began to carry bottles of champagne which they would open upon landing, and share with the farmers. Champagne was good French wine,

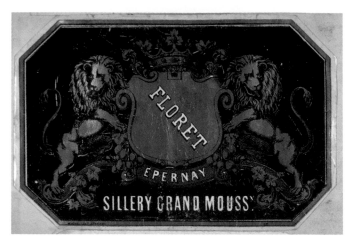

A champagne label with a marketing objective: to identify champagne with the nobility. This one dates from around 1840.

A champagne from around 1880, with a political statement about bringing together the people of France and England.

Severin Roesen, *Still Life with Champagne Bottle and Fruit*, c. 1858.

after all, and had to be respected – and so it followed that the
farmers would honour the French balloonists. This was the
beginning of identifying champagne with glamorous types of
sports and transportation.

Champagne was pictured at horse races, and in scenes of
hunting, rowing and other sporting pursuits of the wealthy
classes. The bourgeoisie embraced this image, purchasing
champagne as a way to associate themselves with the aristocracy. Whenever they could afford to splurge on a celebration,
they bought champagne for personal and professional milestones. As long as status remained aspirational for most of
the world, champagne was the wine of choice, for whoever
could afford it.

In the latter half of the nineteenth century, producers
were able to broaden their range of products, having gained
an increased understanding of the process of making champagne. They began producing and marketing different styles

and qualities of champagne, targeted at specific markets. Champagne Mumm, for example, made several styles of champagne in the 1880s: Cordon Rouge was its driest, Carte Blanche was the sweetest and Extra Dry came in the middle of the range. At this time, wines were also marketed differently for different genders: women were supposed to drink the sweet sparkling wines of Champagne, while men were encouraged to prefer drier champagnes.

4
Sparkling Wine Producers Around the World

By the end of the nineteenth century winemakers in dozens of wine regions around the world were producing sparkling wine called 'champagne'. Some of it was very good, but the sparkling wine producers of Champagne claimed true champagne could only be made in the Champagne region of France. Any other sparkling wine was just sparkling wine. It was not champagne and it was not to be called champagne. In 1878 they began to fight worldwide use of the term 'champagne' as a generic term. Four years later, they formed the Union des Maisons de Champagne or Union of Champagne Houses (UMC), a self-regulating body that exists to this day with one of its stated goals being to 'Prevent the "Champagne" name from being misused across the world'.

In the 1890s, Crimean producers had invited French winemakers to make a type of sparkling wine there. This became well known as *Shampanskoye*, under a variety of brand names. One of the UMC's most important cases occurred in 1904 when the Russian government forced an Odessa company to stop fraudulently using the words 'Roederer' and 'Champagne' on its sparkling wine. This meant that outside of France, the brands and the name of champagne had precedents for their protection.

Impelled by Mumm and Heidsieck, two of the most influential champagne houses, the UMC was able to liaise with the French diplomatic corps to receive timely information about alleged infractions in the sparkling wine world. Through a combination of legal challenges and diplomacy, producers in Champagne continued to guard their name. They also began to create the concept of champagne as a *terroir*-based wine, not simply a winemaking process.

Ever since, the UMC has diligently hunted down other sparkling wine producers in order to stop the widespread (and incorrect, they claim) use of the term 'champagne' on sparkling wine labels. They have taken some producers to court; they have begged, pleaded and cajoled; and in recent years have been successful at forging treaties limiting the use of the name 'champagne' to quality-delimited wines made in Champagne. Today, the EU endorses the *terroir*-based term 'champagne'.

Naming rules aside, during the late nineteenth and early twentieth centuries, excellent sparkling wine was being produced in areas of France such as Burgundy, Alsace and the Loire, and in other European countries, notably Germany, Spain and northern Italy. European settlers in Australia, America and South Africa produced their own versions of sparkling wine from a variety of grapes – along with other fruits, depending on what was available.

As far as the sparkling wine producers of Champagne were concerned, these foreign producers were imitators taking advantage of the great reputation and quality of 'true champagne'. But the foreign producers didn't see how Champagne could have a monopoly on the name of a sparkling wine. Wasn't this a case of imitation being the sincerest form of flattery? The Champagne producers were not flattered, especially not when – as happened all too often in the early years – the alleged 'champagne' was not good wine. It varied widely in quality and style. There were basically three types of spark ling wine producers outside of Champagne. Some producers were making champagne-like wine, usually basing their sparkling wines on the same grapes. Others optimized the potential of their own region's grapes and *terroir* to create their own best possible sparkling wines.

A third group, especially prevalent in the early days of worldwide production, just tried to make anything fizzy that they could sell. In many parts of the world little was known about champagne beyond its fizz and its reputation. Without being able to grow traditional wine grapes in most of the US, some early wine producers there made sparkling wine from many sources, including native American grapes. Still wines from these grapes were said to have a sweet, floral taste at best and a 'foxy' quality at worst. But there was a demand for 'champagne', so unscrupulous producers made sparkling beverages with whatever they could find. English author Charles Dickens, touring America in 1842, found that some of this alleged champagne was made from such far-fetched ingredients as sweetened turnips. Back in his home country, British producers also used whatever they had to hand, one even entering a sparkling wine made from rhubarb in the Great Exhibition of 1851. In America, the sparkling wine situation improved by the end of the nineteenth century, with the development of better-quality vineyards in northern New York state and new wine grape vineyards in California, as well as increased investment in the traditional method of champagne-style production. In England, it would be more than a century before producers successfully planted wine grapes and began to make noteworthy sparkling wines.

Most of the sparkling wine producers in European wine regions had much better resources, and they could grow traditional wine grapes as well. Burgundy, the Loire, Alsace and the Jura are all northern wine-growing regions like Champagne, and they produce champagne-like wines. Burgundy, for example, is directly south of Champagne, and traditionally grows mainly chardonnay and pinot noir grapes. In the 1820s, the prominent Burgundian merchant family Petiot-Groffier hired a producer from Champagne to make sparkling wine. They wanted it to be as similar to champagne as possible so they called it 'Fleur de Champagne' and began to market it in 1826. Fleur de Champagne was advertised in Paris and other large cities as similar to champagne in quality but less expensive. In a few years they were selling 5 million bottles annually. Other producers from Burgundy jumped in, some calling their wines *bourgogne mousseux* (fizzy or foamy burgundy), selling in France and exporting as far as the US, Asia and Africa by the turn of the twentieth century.

In the 1800s, a number of German families immigrated to Champagne and founded champagne houses. They may have already been familiar with this style of winemaking, because Germany's sparkling wine production was well-established. In fact, proprietors of *sektkellerei* (sparkling wine cellars) had imported winemakers from Champagne as early as the 1820s. The Austrian sparkling wine industry is similar to Germany's in that the wine is also called sekt; it began in the mid-1800s.

Sparkling wines are abundant in northern Italy, and often take their names from their region of origin, as with wines from Asti, Aqui Terme (which produces brachetto d'Aqui), Franciacorta, Lambrusco and Prosecco. Most probably, fizzy wines had occurred naturally in these areas for centuries, as they had in France; Brescia's wines were known as such in the Middle Ages. From the mid-nineteenth century on, due to the increased availability of more modern winemaking techniques, and driven at least in part by the popularity of champagne, winemakers in these regions have used their

Early tools for making sparkling wine on display at the Fitz-Ritter cellars – one of the most important *sektkellerei* of the Pfalz area of Germany.

area's wine grapes to produce unique regional styles of sparkling wines.

Italian winemakers brought their sparkling wine traditions to several South American countries when large numbers of emigrants landed in Brazil and Argentina in the late nineteenth and early twentieth centuries. Chile's sparkling wine industry also began in the late 1800s, when pinot noir was planted in Viña Valdivieso's vineyards, and a champagne expert was imported to craft a sparkling wine.

In the New World, California and Australia became important players early on. In the US, German and Italian immigrants led the way. Around Cincinnati, Ohio, German immigrants loved the sparkling wine created by a winemaker from Champagne employed by wine entrepreneur Nicholas Longworth in 1842. Made with native Catawba grapes, the wine's fame touched off a torrent of vineyard plantings in the region as its consumption spread to the East Coast where

Labels for sparkling wine produced in the 19th century by predecessors of the Fitz-Ritter winery in Germany. At that time, their sparkling wine was sometimes called Moussirender.

A 19th-century German 'Champagne' poster advertising wines from the Fitz & Baust Schaumweinkellerei, meaning 'foamy wine cellars'.

even those accustomed to European wines enjoyed it. In the US, famed poet Henry Wadsworth Longfellow wrote an 'Ode to Catawba Wine', comparing it favourably to wines from Champagne, Germany and Spain. In Britain, Robert Browning liked the wine, and a reporter for the *Illustrated London News* thought it was better than champagne. Even the French scientist Jules-Émile Planchon declared sparkling Catawba wine was excellent when he toured Midwestern vineyards in 1873.

Several of the earliest sparkling wine producers are still in business today, mainly producing high-volume but lower-quality wines. In addition to the Midwest and California, wineries in upstate (northern) New York State also proliferated in the nineteenth century. Founded as Pleasant Valley Wine Company in New York State in 1860, the Great Western Winery began taking medals in Europe as early as 1867 for its 'American Champagne'. Inglenook, Cook's Imperial Champagne Cellars and Korbel Champagne Cellars started to produce 'Champagne' in California in the latter half of the nineteenth century. In Northern California, a German immigrant, Jacob Schram, bought a piece of land in Napa in 1862 where he established what would become California's first all-sparkling winery, well known today as Schramsberg.

Even farther from Champagne, Joseph Seppelt, a Polish immigrant to Australia, founded a winery in 1851 in Victoria and began to make sparkling wine; Seppelt's winery is famous for traditionally made sparkling wine today. Australia's popular red sparkling shiraz has been made since the 1860s.

How Champagne and Sparkling Wine Are Made

By the end of the nineteenth century, the production process for sparkling wine in Champagne had stabilized. The same method was used to make quality sparkling wines in other areas of the world – especially those regions that grew the same grapes. This was known as the Champagne Method (*méthode champenoise*). Today, the word 'champagne' has been replaced; it is now known as the traditional method (*méthode traditionelle*, also termed *méthode classique* or *méthode traditionelle classique*). These words on a label are an important indicator of the quality of the wine in the bottle.

The sparkling wine production process involves many intricate and exacting steps, and has changed little since the latter part of the 1800s, beginning in geographically defined vineyards, cultivated to have specified yields. Every year, the grapes for champagne are harvested by hand, at a precise point of ripeness that emphasizes certain flavours and acidic

Harvesting grapes in Champagne, in the Montaigne de Reims area.

components of the grape – not the maximum ripeness and sugar as for other table wines. Red grapes have to be completely whole and unblemished or their skins will colour the white champagnes, so the grapes must be handled very carefully at all times. Formerly, grape presses might be brought out to the fields but now the harvested grape bunches are carefully placed in shallow bins so the grapes are not crushed while being conveyed to the winery. There the grapes are destemmed, pressed in the prescribed manner in special, gentle presses, and the must (grape juice) is put into vats to ferment.

Most producers ferment each parcel – part or all of each vineyard – separately. Often commercially grown yeasts are added to begin fermentation. Some yeasts are strains isolated from the vineyards and grown in laboratories, while others are independently designed and grown for use in champagnes. Commercial yeasts assure consistency in fermentation and contribute to the flavour profile of the sparkling wine. Occasionally certain producers use the indigenous yeasts from the vineyards; this determination is made by each winery.

When the grapes are being pressed, yeasts found on the skins mix with the grape juice and they will eventually begin a natural fermentation. But when added, commercial yeasts are stronger, and they eclipse the indigenous yeasts.

The yeasts die off after consuming the sugars in the grapes and turning them into alcohol. Since these grapes are slightly less ripe at harvest, there is a little less sugar in them than in grapes harvested later in the season for table wines, so the resultant champagne has a lower alcohol level, a few per cent less than table wines today.

Fermentation typically occurs over the course of about ten days at cool temperatures (around $64-8°$ F or $18-20°$ C). Most of today's champagne vats are stainless steel, and temperature-controlled. A few producers ferment their wines in oak vats of varying sizes, and these can contribute specific flavours to the finished wines. A number of winemakers then allow some or all of their vats to warm up – or mechanically bring them up to a certain temperature – to induce a second fermentation known as malolactic. Among other things, they believe this makes the finished wine smoother and creamier at an earlier age.

The wines are then left to mature until spring, sometime in March or April, when the blending (*assemblage*) begins. Traditionally, champagne houses have signature styles which they maintain year after year, and which require specialized blending. Some of the still wine from previous years is allowed in these blends. Before blending, any vats that are judged sub-par can be rejected, and the wines may be sold off.

In large champagne houses, there are dozens, occasionally hundreds, of separately fermented vats of wines. When the blend is decided on, the wines are gently mixed together in giant vats. At this point they are all still wines (not sparkling) because the CO_2, a by-product of fermentation, has not been

captured. Now, the wines must undergo a second fermenta
tion, so the *liqueur de tirage* is added to start it. *Liqueur de tirage*
consists of still wine with yeast and additional sugar for the
yeast to consume, to initiate the fermentation process. The
wine is bottled and sealed with a very prosaic crown cap (like
a beer-bottle top). After scientist Louis Pasteur figured out
how the yeasts worked in the winemaking process in 1857, it
still took years of trials to figure out the correct proportions
in a *liqueur de tirage*. Professor Edouard Robinet of Epernay
was the first to define and use this term in 1877; the process
became more common after that.

The bottles are placed on their sides on wooden racks or
pallets in the cool, underground chalk cellars in Champagne.
There they rest for a period ranging from a few weeks to many
years while the beneficial process of autolysis can take place
– the yeast cells break down and certain elements are absorbed

Barrels of still wine ageing in the cellar at Vilmart et Cie in Champagne
before it undergoes a secondary fermentation to become sparkling wine.

by the wine. During this time, the lees (dead yeast cells and other solid matter in the wine) also slowly drift to the bottom (actually the side of the bottle, to begin with). These developments add nuances of flavour and fragrance, including aromas like yeasty bread and toastiness to the finished wine.

Traditionally the bottles are then placed in wooden riddling racks. Every day, a riddler (*remueur*) goes through the cellar, one section at a time, rotating each bottle a fraction of a turn, and pushing it back into the rack. An experienced riddler can rotate thousands of bottles a day. After a period of six to twelve weeks the bottles have also gradually been placed at a greater and greater angle so that they are nearly vertical, upside down. The combination of shifting the angle and slightly jarring the bottle makes the lees slide down into the neck. Nowadays, most champagne and sparkling wine producers do this by machine, placing hundreds of bottles in large, square wire cages where they are moved mechanically, and the whole process takes a fraction of the time – only a little over a week. These large, mechanically turning machines have various names depending on their manufacturer, but are commonly called gyropalettes – the most common ones hold 504 bottles per cage. Today, only a few traditionalists like Pol Roger use riddlers, as most champagne producers believe that gyropalettes are just as effective.

The next step is the process of taking the wine off the lees: this is done as 'frozen disgorgement' (*dégorgement à la glace*); it was developed in 1884 and is done the same way today. The bottles of sparkling wine are kept upside down while they wait for disgorging. The tip of each upside-down bottle is placed in chilled salt-water at -18°F (-28°C) so the neck is essentially flash-frozen. Immediately, the bottle's crown cap is pried off and the lees shoot out in a solid plug, along with a minimal amount of wine. Then the dosage is added to the bottle, to

Riddling racks in a champagne cave, with just enough room for the riddler to slip between them.

correct flavours and ensure the bottle is at the correct fill level. The dosage, also known as *liqueur d'expédition*, is a proprietary recipe for each winemaker, but consists of some amount of sugar mixed with alcohol spirits (initially with cognac to strengthen the alcohol of the sweeter champagnes). Then a large cylindrical cork is quickly compressed and crammed into the bottle. The upper part of the cork, uncompressed, blooms out over the bottle, giving champagne its characteristic bulbous topping. After that, a foil label is wrapped around the curved top of the cork and the neck of the bottle. A wire cage (*muselet*) secures the cork when the bottom pieces of the wire cage are twisted closed around a glass lip manufactured into the neck of the bottle. After front and back labels are applied, the champagne is rested for a short while before it is shipped out to the world, ready to drink.

Vintage champagnes are created only in years when the grapes are of the highest quality and the wines will age very

Workers in a champagne cellar performing the dangerous job of hand-disgorging champagne, when errant corks would sometimes fly off in the wrong direction, and bottles would suddenly shatter. Nowadays, this process is done by machine.

Champagne corks, such as these from Amorim, are larger in diameter than those for table wine bottles. They are compressed more when inserted, and they retain a mushroom shape when released from the bottle.

well; they are a wonderful accident of nature which occurs, on average, a few times a decade. For a vintage wine, only the wines made with grapes from that specific year's harvest can be used. Vintage champagnes may be kept longer in the cellars. They are only released when they are at a peak of quality for drinking – though certain vintage champagnes may last many more years in the bottle. Many vintage champagnes are 'late disgorged', which means they stay on the lees for many years before their final bottling.

There are other production methods as well, mostly used for lesser-quality sparkling wines, and not in Champagne houses. For example, some wine is kept in a large vat instead of in individual bottles during the wine's secondary fermentation. This is known as the charmat or bulk process. For this method, the secondary fermentation happens in a pressurized tank, and the wine is bottled under pressure, as well.

Champagne bottles up-ended at the finish of the riddling process.

The wine does not stay in contact with the lees, and the result is a less complex – and less expensive – wine. However, charmat is the best method for wines made from certain grapes, like prosecco, which are negatively affected by extended contact with the lees.

Another process, known as the transfer method, was devised as an attempt to do away with the time-consuming riddling. After the secondary fermentation is completed in bottles, the bottles are opened and the wines poured out into a tank, where the lees are settled out before the finished wine is re-bottled. It is less time-consuming and less expensive – and, when the wines are treated in bulk, the result is lesser-quality sparkling wines. It became less worthwhile once the large riddling machines (gyropalettes) were invented.

Even less expensive and poorer-quality sparkling wine is made with a variety of bulk-production techniques, such as the quick 'Russian continuous method', where the still wine is passed through several tanks during a period of days. The first tanks have yeast and sugar in them to induce a secondary fermentation while the wine goes through, and the last tanks are for filtering and clarifying the sparkling wine before bottling. This allows very little wine to come into contact with the flavour- and aroma-enhancing lees, producing a much less interesting product. The most minimal production method for sparkling wine is to merely inject carbonation into a still wine, resulting in a rather monochromatic sparkling beverage.

Artisanal production methods are most often used today to preserve the feel of early sparkling wine. Called ancestral, artisanal and rural (*méthode ancestrale*, *méthode artisanale* and *méthode rurale*) they refer to the early, single-fermentation method for making sparkling wine – the way it occurred naturally, centuries ago.

5

Wars, Society and Taste: Stresses on Champagne in the Twentieth Century

At the beginning of the twentieth century champagne was famous worldwide. Wasn't this exactly what the champagne producers wanted? Yes and no. While everyone wished to have champagne for celebrations, not everyone could afford it. This gave rise to local sparkling wine industries that flourished not only because of cost and distance issues, but because many of them were using the same grapes and quality production methods as in Champagne. Very good sparkling wines could be made in other regions of the world. This hit Champagne especially hard during times of conflict and depression throughout the century. However, persevering with their promotions, champagne producers were able to increase demand for their sparkling wines so much that towards the end of the century they began looking elsewhere for more good vineyard land – to make sparkling wine outside Champagne. Several champagne houses established satellite wineries in localities with reputable wine regions such as California, Australia and Argentina. In addition, champagne producers began to float shocking concepts such as increasing

A poster advertising the allure of champagne – the romance and the glory – designed by Walter Crane in a classic belle epoque style, 1894.

the designated area for champagne production in France, and looking at land across the Channel in England where there was a continuation of the chalk and limestone soil that grew great grapes in Champagne.

Economic stresses on twentieth-century Champagne began in the early part of the century when two devastating world wars raged through the region. During the First World War, residents periodically retreated into the Champagne caves or cellars for safety, and whole communities lived there while shelling went on overhead. The producers tried to continue selling champagne to maintain their livelihoods, while also attempting to protect their vineyards and wine from plundering armies. At the same time they were completing the arduous task of uprooting their vines and replanting them on American rootstock – the only remedy for the phylloxera grapevine epidemic that had been ravaging European vineyards for decades.

As Champagne was not too far from Germany (and borders fluctuated over time), personal loyalties to France sometimes came into question during the wars. Army conscription problems arose in families of winemakers and businessmen who originally came from Germany to produce champagne and had lived in France for generations without bothering to become French citizens. This happened in 1914 to Hermann von Mumm, whose family had been in France since 1827; he was interned in Brittany and the French government took over Champagne Mumm.

When Germany controlled the area, their army drank copious amounts of champagne wherever they found it. Though producers walled up as many bottles as they could, sometimes these treasure troves were discovered by the soldiers. After the Great War, the whole commercial landscape of Europe changed, with the evaporation both of the Austro-Hungarian

Empire and Tsarist Russia with their many royal customers. And there was also a lot less champagne to sell: vineyards and even whole villages had been destroyed by bombing, gassing and other acts of destruction. This war was so horrific that the Armistice is still marked emotionally every year, in every village in the Champagne region on the eleventh hour of the eleventh day of the eleventh month.

Both before and after the war, copious amounts of sparkling wine were produced in Russia with the bulk method and continuous method; they were made from native grapes as well as imported must and wine. Russia's most famous sparkling wine company, Abrau-Durso, had brought in a Frenchman to oversee their 'champagne-making' in the 1890s, and the company has continued to produce sparkling wine they proudly call 'Sovetskoye Shampanskoye' to this day. In the early Stalinist years, champagne fell into disfavour because it was considered elitist. Suddenly, in 1936, the government decided that Russia needed to show off the success of its government and lifestyle, and government-sanctioned 'champagne' production became a priority, along with other luxuries such as fine boxes of candies and tins of caviar. Production increased and became more industrialized after new facilities were established near the Soviet Union's largest cities; only a few urbanites could actually afford 'Soviet Champagne' though all citizens were encouraged to buy it for weddings and other celebrations.

For French champagne, business began to improve when the Roaring Twenties carried champagne to new heights of fame in Europe and the UK. Across the Atlantic, Prohibition shut down the US market from 1920 to 1933 – except for a few bold bootleggers who smuggled champagne in from the Caribbean and Canada for moneyed clientele. Then the Great Depression further took its toll on Champagne.

Poster advertising *Sovetskoye Shampanskoye* or Soviet Champagne, 'the best grape wine', 1952.

This early 20th-century poster promises the glamour of Paris and Eros in a bottle.

The Second World War revved up the US economy, but to the French it was a horrible déjà vu as fighting once again stormed through the region of Champagne. Demand for champagne was down, and shipping was nearly impossible. Champagne producers had to find a balance between the imperative of making a living and the personal and political cost of supplying top customers who now ruled Germany, their enemy. Berlin requisitioned thousands of bottles per month – and the German regime did pay something for the wine. And during the Second World War, the countryside fared better than in the First World War as more vineyards and villages were spared. It was still a dark time for the French, with very little in the way of supplies or manpower for vineyard care, harvests and wine production. Finally, at the end of the war, there was a bit of poetic justice: Allied Commander (later US President) Eisenhower signed the treaty ending the Second World War in Reims, in the heart of Champagne.

The Champagne Riots of 1911. Grape-growers protested new decreases in the official growing area of Champagne. They won a partial reversal then, and a full re-incorporation in 1927.

Before and after the wars, champagne producers continued the campaign to protect their *terroir*-based name and define the vineyard areas where grapes for champagne could be grown. Their first challenge had come in 1908 when the French government declared that only two *départements* (county-type areas), Marne and Aisne, could grow champagne. Historically, a third *département*, Aube, had been part of the Champagne commercial region for centuries. The growers of Aube protested but the French laws only became stricter so in 1911 they staged a violent 'Champagne Rebellion'. The laws were then amended to classify Aube – along with Seine-et-Marne – as a secondary champagne zone, but in 1927 the two areas were re-incorporated into champagne-making territory. These boundaries remained in place until very recently.

Even with their guarantees of quality, the sparkling wine producers of Champagne faced increasing competition from other sparkling wine makers who were becoming well-established in many areas of the world. Champagne producers had to keep their wine in the limelight, continually touting its quality and cachet. Persistent campaigns with periodic anniversary celebrations, alliances with cultural institutions and pop-cultural figures, the film business and fashion moguls have contributed significantly to champagne's upscale and oh-so-desirable image.

One of the most successful was Moët et Chandon's creation of their Dom Pérignon champagne. The original champagne promotion association from 1882, Syndicat du Commerce des Vins de Champagne, later became the Syndicat de Grandes Marques. In 1932, this group decided, rather arbitrarily, to hold celebrations of the 250th anniversary of Dom Pérignon's 'invention' of champagne at Hautvillers Abbey. An advisor suggested creating a special, high-priced blend of champagne for the occasion. Though it didn't happen then, a few years later, Moët et Chandon's managing director, Count de Vogue, decided to produce his own special 'Dom Pérignon' sparkling wine, vintage 1921. He made it in honour of the 100th anniversary of Simon Brothers of London, Moët's exclusive agent in Britain. He also packaged it in a replica eighteenth-century bottle, and had the cork tied on with string secured by green wax. Its shield-shaped label with vine motif had been used by Moët et Chandon during Napoleon's time. In Britain, Simon Brothers gave 300 bottles of this first 'Cuvée Dom Pérignon' to their best customers. The first 100 cases of Dom Pérignon arrived in the USA in December 1936. Dom Pérignon has since become the most famous champagne around the world for high-end celebrations. No top restaurant anywhere in the world can now have a wine list without a bottle of 'Dom'.

The champagne producers continued their promotion and protection campaigns. In 1942 the name of their association became Union des Maisons de Champagne (UMC). Some of the smaller houses formed an association in 1943 that also worked with the UMC until 1994 when both groups merged under the UMC name. Today there are about 100 members who primarily blend grapes to produce their own, consistent house styles of champagne. This includes the major champagne houses – the most famous, established brands, known as the Grandes Marques. It does not include the grower-producers who make wine from their own grapes – a much smaller group, which is on the rise today.

At the end of the Second World War, the third of the great widows of champagne (after Veuve Clicquot and Louise Pommery) took her place in history: Elizabeth 'Lily' Bollinger. One of champagne's loveliest quotes is attributed to her:

Mme Bollinger on her trademark bicycle in the Champagne countryside, 1960s.

> I only drink champagne when I'm happy, or when
> I'm sad.
> I sometimes drink it when I'm alone.
> When I have company, I consider it obligatory.
> I trifle with it if I am not hungry and drink it when I am.
> Otherwise I never touch it – unless I'm thirsty.

Lily had taken over Bollinger when her husband died in 1941, and after the war was the first to visit Britain and the United States to re-energize her brand – and incidentally, champagne in general. Lily Bollinger was also the first to produce the sparkling wine she labelled RD (for *récemment dégorgé*), which means that the wine had been kept on the lees longer, and disgorged later, to add complexity and depth to its flavours and aromas. The first Bollinger RD was vintage 1952, released in 1961. This practice has been followed by other producers; the champagnes are now called 'late disgorged'.

Though champagne had occasional struggles in the world-wide economy well into the 1970s, the large champagne houses continued to specialize in blending grapes for their own signature styles of sparkling wines, and they could call the shots on the prices they paid for grapes. The hundreds of village vineyards had been ranked, starting at the top with *grand cru*, then *premier cru*, then *village* vineyards. These quality gradations were mirrored in the prices paid for the grapes. There was a certain amount of resentment among the growers, but they could do very little about it without the resources to make their own champagnes. In Champagne, the champagne houses ruled.

Elsewhere, it was another story. After the mid-twentieth century when the middle class had grown and become more financially secure, a new economic genre arose, the aspirationally affluent. Both of these groups embraced champagne's luxury positioning. They saw themselves as part of champagne's

In France, the term crémant now refers to sparkling wine made outside the Champagne region. This is a sign at the entrance to the crémant region of Burgundy.

Burgundy is a northern wine region like Champagne. Sparkling wine has been produced in Burgundy since the 1800s. This is an early sign advertising a type of sparkling wine called Chablis Mousseux, made by one of the most notable producers in the Chablis region of Burgundy.

targeted upscale market. They wanted to drink more sparkling wine even if they couldn't always afford champagne. Certain sparkling wine makers took notice of aspirational champagne buyers and they flooded the market with cheap, sweet sparklers like 'pink champagne' and Cold Duck. Gradually these products lost out to the increasingly sophisticated taste of the middle and upper middle classes who travelled and learned more about food and wine. During the late twentieth century, producers in many established wine regions around the world began to upgrade their sparkling wine making, and to aim their products at this new group of more savvy customers. In Burgundy, for example, quality had varied for many decades until controls were put in place in 1943, with the creation of a 'Bourgogne Mousseux' appellation, which defined the vineyard area and production quality of these wines. In the 1970s, a group of producers instituted further quality controls for their vines, vineyards and wines, and were instrumental in establishing the new sparkling wine appellation (Appellation d'Origine Contrôllée, or AOC), 'Crémant de Bourgogne' in 1975.

In the Loire Valley, the Crémant de Loire AOC was also created in 1975, around Saumur and extending into the Touraine and Anjou wine regions. The sparkling wines from the Crémant de Loire appellation are made with traditional Loire grapes rather than those used in Champagne. Also, more than half of the Loire's Vouvray AOC wines are sparkling, made from chenin blanc. The Loire Valley is currently the second largest producer of sparkling wines in France.

Before 1990, *crémant* (creamily foamy) referred to a wine that was less fizzy, under less pressure than champagne. Crémant is now the term for quality French sparkling wines made outside of Champagne. It is a restricted term, and can only be given to wines from AOCs including Crémant de Bourgogne, Crémant d'Alsace and Crémant de Loire in the north; Crémant de Jura and Crémant de Bordeaux in the middle of France; Crémant de Limoux in the south; and Crémant de Die to the east of the Rhone. There is also a Crémant de Luxembourg in this adjacent country. Many of these wines are produced with lower pressure than champagne – they are a bit less fizzy – but they are made in the same traditional method and, as in champagne, all the grapes must be hand-harvested.

Sparkling wine production and distribution is growing in all regions. In Alsace, for example, Crémant d'Alsace production increased from a million bottles in 1979 to 33 million in 2008, and it now comprises 22 per cent of Alsatian wine. Crémant d'Alsace is a well-crafted, lower-priced competitor to champagne; it is made with Alsatian grapes either individually or in a blend; the blanc de blancs, sparkling wine made with white grapes only, is most often only made with pinot blanc while a rosé is usually pinot noir.

There are a few exceptions to the 'crémant' name for French sparkling wine. The historic Limoux region of France, which has been making sparkling wine since the 1500s, now produces three types of wine. Crémant de Limoux brut is made primarily with chardonnay and chenin blanc, with smaller amounts of mauzac blanc and pinot noir. Blanquette de Limoux is a sparkling brut made with the traditional mauzac grape and up to 10 per cent chenin blanc and chardonnay. La Blanquette Méthode Ancéstrale is made from the mauzac grape, with the original, single-fermentation process. In Die, there is a modern, brut Crémant de Die as well as Clairette de Die, a sparkling wine that has been in production since the Gauls lived in this region of south-eastern France nearly 2,000 years ago; it is made from the clairette grape blended with muscat and aligoté.

In Germany, sekt can refer to a cheap and cheerful sparkler often made with imported still wine in bulk processes. Perlwein is another popular, inexpensive German wine, lightly sparkling, whose quality has lately been improving. Deutscher sekt wines are produced from German-grown grapes in any region. Many grapes, both German and international varietals, can be used, including riesling, silvaner, pinot blanc and pinot gris, huxelrebe, gewürztraminer and pinot noir. In wines labelled *Sekt b.A.* or *Qualitätsschaumwein b.A.* that list the region and sometimes the vineyard, 85 per cent of the grapes must be from the place(s) stated on the label. Some of this wine is estate-produced while a fair amount is made for German wineries at a contract facility; regardless, these are finer wines now than they have been in the past.

In Austria, most sparkling wine is made with native Austrian grapes, mainly the welschriesling and grüner veltliner that are grown primarily in the north-east corner of the Weinviertel near the borders of the Czech Republic and Slovakia. International grape varietals can also be used in Austria's sekt, which can be made in many styles – with red as well as white grapes. In Burgenland, a more southern Austrian wine region near the Hungarian border, several wineries specialize in producing a sparkling red from the zweigelt grape or from pinot noir.

Many sparkling wines are made in Italy's northern regions, such as Asti, Brachetto d'Aqui, Franciacorta, Lambrusco and Prosecco. Though these wines have respectable origins, during the mid-twentieth century careless and disreputable producers ruined the reputations of many of these regions by over-producing sparkling wines of very low quality. Often the wines were sweet and unbalanced, the cloying flavours driving another nail into their coffins. Happily, during the past decade or so, producers put into place quality restrictions for every aspect of the wine from vines to vinification. They have a lot to overcome but their hard work is beginning to pay off. One region even chose to rename its quality wines in order to change public perception: formerly asti spumante, the better wines are now simply termed 'asti'. In some instances Italian wine producers are struggling to overcome long memories of early export advertising by specific companies. In the US, radio jingles like the rhyming 'Martini and Rossi, Asti Spumante' still play in many consumers' heads, referencing an inexpensive, sweet sparkler marketed for the holidays since the 1960s. One wine from Lambrusco has been so overexposed many people believe 'Cella Lambrusco' is the name of the region; they are unaware that it refers only to the specific brand of sparkling wine made by Fratelli Cella. The reputation of Italian sparkling wine also still suffers in the UK, though there are signs it is on a slow road to recovery there, too.

In Emilia Romagna and Lombardy, several Lambrusco DOCs (Denominazione di Origine Controllata) are made with red lambrusco grapes and blends. So far, these wines have not overcome the mid-twentieth century damage to their reputations, at least not outside of their home region. Neither has Lombardy's Franciacorta region, which achieved DOCG (Denominazione di Origine Controllata e Garantita) status in 1995, producing sparkling wines from chardonnay blended with *pinot bianco* (pinot blanc) and *pinot nero* (pinot noir) grapes. Franciacorta DOCG wines include the white Bianco Spumante Classico and Crémant Spumante Classico and a rosé, Rosato Spumante Classico, all made in the traditional method, aged from 25 to 37 months. Satén was originally a proprietary name but is now used as a local term for the sparkling wine made exclusively from chardonnay; satén rosé has a minimum of 15 per cent pinot nero.

Prosecco, in Italy, is a sterling example of hard work by winemakers who, from the beginning, strove to maximize the potential of their native prosecco grape in their own sparkling wine. The prosecco grape must be handled in almost the opposite manner from traditional champagne grapes. In order to preserve the lively acidity that contributes freshness to the finished sparkling wine, prosecco must immediately be removed from the lees – leaving prosecco on the lees muddies the flavours and texture of the wine. In the 1920s, the pressurized tank the Italians call *autoclave* was perfected. Once the prosecco has undergone its second fermentation, it is taken off the lees and kept in a pressurized *autoclave* and prosecco producers can bottle their wine as needed, throughout the year. In the spirit of the great champagne houses, they endeavour to keep their quality and flavours consistent. During the last few months of the remaining wine, usually January through March, prosecco producers blend the last

The Prosecco region has many hillside vineyards. This is Farra di Soligo, one of the communes of the highest quality wine, prosecco DOCG Conegliano Valdobbiadene.

vintage with the new vintage so no one who customarily drinks their preferred brand of prosecco gets too much of a shock to their palate.

Spain, the second largest sparkling wine producer in Europe, has produced large amounts of sparkling wine since Josep Raventós i Fatjó began commercial production in 1872. Within five years, Spanish *Xampán* (champagne) was the only sparkling wine served at the Spanish court. The dread vine disease phylloxera began to destroy French vineyards around this time, so many French wine producers looked to Spain for their grapes and their wine. With its exports, Spanish sparkling wine production quickly became profitable. This sparkler later became known as cava.

Heavily regulated, cava production received DO (Denominación de Origen) status in 1986. Eighty-five per cent of Spanish cava is made in the north-eastern part of Spain around Barcelona; a much smaller amount is made in the non-adjacent Rioja region in north-central Spain. Cava is made in the traditional method, but mainly with the Spanish grapes macabeo, xarel-lo, parellada and subirat. *Garnacha* (grenache) and *monastrell* (mourvèdre) are also permitted, and in rosé cavas pinot noir and trepat can also be used. Cava is a relatively young, fresh wine, blended a few months after harvest, aged on the lees for a minimum of nine months. For the past few decades, Spanish sparkling wines have gained favour in many countries because of their lower cost and reasonable quality; recent regulatory requirements in Spanish wine-making have driven up quality as well as price. The famous 'black bottle' of the Freixenet brand was one of the first to exhibit quality as well as creating favourable awareness of Spain among sparkling wine consumers in the United States, while consumers in Britain had long had Spanish wines available to them at very good prices.

Due to South Africa's remote location, its sparkling wine producers have been little known outside of their own country. Their first sparkling wine was called *Kaapse Vonkel*, which

Mechanized bottling of cava, the Spanish quality sparkling wine.

Hand-crafted giant barrels used in the production of cava, Spanish sparkling wine.

A bus from the early 20th century advertising Freixenet, one of Spain's premier cavas.

means 'Cape Sparkle'. In creating the current term 'Cap Classique' for sparkling wine produced using the traditional methods of the Champagne region, South African producers were honouring a 1935 trade agreement with France. In 1992, the country's sparkling wine producers formed an association that regulates quality and promotes the wines.

In the Western hemisphere, Brazil's sparkling wines are little known outside Brazil though the industry dates from 1875; the wines are traditionally made with the muscat grape. Chilean pioneer sparkling wine producer Viña Valdivieso has prospered for more than a century and produces over 60 per cent of the country's mainly holiday-related sparkling wine. The situation in Argentina is similar in that the largest market is domestic, though exports are growing. In addition to long-time regional producers, two champagne houses, Mumm and Moët et Chandon, have established wineries in Argentina, and now make a significant proportion of the country's sparkling wine.

Several of the earliest sparkling wine producers in the United States are still in business today, though there is a big gap in wine history in the United States. At the beginning of the twentieth century, just as production, interstate transportation and demand were growing steadily, the temperance movement was also gaining momentum. The result was Prohibition, a fourteen-year period from 1919 to 1933 during which the production and consumption of alcohol was prohibited in the US. There were few exceptions, notably medicinal and religious. Another little loophole allowed home winemakers to produce a small amount of wine for their own home consumption. These tiny exceptions were all that kept (legal) US winemaking alive. Some growers in California shipped grapes back east for home winemakers. Others produced extremely modest amounts of wine or spirits for religious ceremonies or medicinal purposes. Paul Masson, a winemaker originally from Burgundy, France, had formed the Paul Masson Champagne Company in California and received acclaim for his wines in the early 1900s. He was only able to keep his winery going during Prohibition by selling grapes and by holding the sole US licence to make 'medicinal champagne'.

After the repeal of Prohibition, there was suddenly a lot of poor-quality sparkling wine for sale. Because wine consumption disappeared for the better part of a generation, Americans lost their habit of drinking wine as well as any confidence in their knowledge of wines. It was simpler to turn to spirits, rather than expensive or questionable sparkling wines. Americans weren't used to spending a lot on wine, so some of the previously known, mass-marketed sparkling wines did well. One of them, Korbel, went as far as to trademark their 'California Champagne' product name in the 1950s.

Sparkling wine makers in certain areas of the country persevered in their quest to produce quality, dry sparkling wines. An early entry into this market was the Davies family, which acquired Jacob Schram's California property in 1965, and they proudly proclaim Schramsberg to be 'America's First House of Sparkling Wine'. Having decided to concentrate on sparkling wines, the Davies family pioneered using traditional champagne grapes in American sparkling wine, and they have continually improved their wines. A pivotal point for them – and for American sparkling wine – came in 1972 when then US President Nixon took Schramsberg sparkling wine to China to serve at a state dinner there.

French champagne houses also expanded into California at that time. In the 1970s, Moët et Chandon bought 800 acres in the Napa Valley to establish Domaine Chandon. In 1980, Piper Sonoma was founded by Champagne house Piper-Heidsieck, and in 1982 Roederer Estate grew out of Louis

Roederer's expansion plans. Mumm Napa launched in 1985 and Domaine Carneros (a Taittinger venture) was founded in 1987.

An eminent sparkling wine making family from Spain, the Ferrers (of Freixenet) bought land in 1982 and opened Gloria Ferrer winery in 1986. In 1991 the other top Spanish cava maker founded Cordoniu Napa, now Artesa, which continues to produce sparkling wine.

Important quality sparkling wine producers in California include J, Iron Horse and Scharffenberger. Sparkling wines from other western wineries such as Argyle in Oregon and Chateau Ste. Michelle in Washington State began to appear first in the west, then in more of the country. Further east a French family founded Gruet in New Mexico. Winemakers in many US states also began to grow grapes and purchase them in order to make wines. There was a long tradition of northern wine production in upper New York State, including sparkling wines. In New England wineries such as Westport

A modern, computerized champagne grape press.

Rivers in Massachusetts began to understand their climate just to the north of the protected waters of Long Island Sound, and to dedicate time and effort to sparkling wines.

The Australians, like the Americans, went through a phase of producing and consuming sweet sparkling wine, often pink, which crested in the 1960s and early '70s. Australia's most popular pink sparkling wine was first called sparkling burgundy, then by its grape name 'sparkling shiraz'. Later, finding a growing market for quality, dry sparkling wines, French champagne houses began investing in Australia in the 1980s. Moët et Chandon, Roederer and Bollinger formed winery partnerships in several of the cooler wine-growing regions.

6

Style, Styles and Stylishness

In the West, educated wine consumers tend to believe every celebration calls for champagne, from launching a ship or a marriage to commemorating an anniversary or a special achievement. With Western culture spreading through television and the Internet, people around the world now subscribe to the belief that champagne is a requirement for public and private events, at home, in restaurants and in nightclubs.

Film stars and musicians became the worldwide royalty of the twentieth and twenty-first centuries. Fans from every country now aspire to the products consumed by these celebrities. Champagne has a long history of stylishness in movies. Cary Grant drank it debonairly in many films, beginning in the 1930s. Betty Grable and Bette Davis sipped it. Spencer Tracy and Katharine Hepburn served it in their movies. Marilyn Monroe had potato chips with her pink champagne. Angelina Jolie drank it onscreen while she seduced Brad Pitt offscreen. The many James Bonds quaffed plenty of champagne – always specifying their brand, usually Bollinger, sometimes Dom Pérignon or Taittinger. Perhaps the most famous film toast of all is Humphrey Bogart's understated champagne tribute to Ingrid Bergman in *Casablanca*: 'Here's looking at you, kid.'

Pierre Bonnard designed this 1891 poster for France-Champagne, another advertisement equating the glamorous lifestyle of *fin-de-siècle* France with sparkling wine from Champagne.

Those seeking to add a touch of glamour to their lives are surrounded by enticing sparkling wine imagery: fashion models sipping champagne from individually sized, brightly coloured Pommery Pop bottles through a straw and sultry singers imbibing it from crystal flutes in music videos. Louis Roederer's Cristal, initially created for the Russian tsars and not produced again until 1945, was then marketed to the upper classes. By the 1990s it was a cult favourite in Hollywood and it became de rigueur for hip-hop artists, wannabes and fans. Until 2006, when a brand representative implied this market might be less than desirable and rapper Jay-Z led the anti-Cristal charge by promoting another champagne he had discovered: Armand de Brignac's Ace of Spades – which could become very well-known in the future.

Dom Pérignon, the world's most famous champagne, with its shield-shaped label and curvaceous bottle.

Champagne's ascendancy has continued in the twenty-first century, with the addition of millions of new consumers in emergent and developing economies. In September 2007 film crews and journalists from the United States, India, China and Russia were crisscrossing the Champagne region, eagerly preparing reports for their home countries about the harvest of this magical sparkling wine. The champagne producers were polite and welcoming to all, but there was a sense that they were more excited about the groups from India, China and Russia: the new markets. There, the 'beautiful people' entertaining in restaurants are toasting each other with champagne for the first time. Brut and rosé champagnes are fashionable in all three, with sweeter champagnes still the preference in Russia. 'Russian champagne' is still popular and continues to be produced in great quantities, most notably by the historic Abrau-Durso company. In India, sales of champagne have grown by 25 per cent a year for the past three years. Champagne now accounts for 10 per cent of the wine sales in the country, while other sparkling wines such as cava and prosecco are now available in Delhi. In Russia, champagne sales were going up five per cent a year before the recent economic downturn, and are expected to pick up again, with luxury brands most in demand by the post-communist wealthy class. In China, the most famous champagne houses have entered the market, pioneered by Veuve Clicquot, Mumm and Ayala. In Russia, China and Thailand, prosecco is taking up the slack where demand for high-end champagnes has fallen off. Driven by the weak economy, in Japan non-vintage champagnes are selling better than vintage and *têtes de cuvée* (top of the line) champagnes. Japan's next bestselling sparkling wine is cava from Spain, followed by sparkling wines from anywhere else in the world, from Argentina to Australia.

In the UK, supermarkets function as a label of trust for many people, and for good reason. The supermarket buyers are extremely knowledgeable about wines and about their customers; they are also experienced in transacting business with wine producers and promoting the producers to the British. In upscale champagne, the British are experienced consumers, having been one of Champagne's first export markets centuries ago. Many prefer vintage champagnes and heartier styles such as Bollinger and Billecart-Salmon, though lighter styles are gaining ground. Price has also become a factor now that more people are consuming sparkling wines regularly rather than waiting for the holidays, and even long-time champagne customers are now more open to buying less expensive sparkling wines from other regions of the world such as Australia, Italy and Spain.

Demand for Italian sparkling wine is increasing in the UK, as it is in the rest of the world. In 2008, UK consumers drank almost twice as much Italian sparkling wine as the year before. The Spanish consumed 88 per cent more and even in Russia, usually considered a French champagne market, sales of Italian sparkling wines rose 40 per cent.

In the twenty-first century, prosecco producers have continued to improve their wines. In August 2009 they were granted the special DOCG Conegliano-Valdobbiadene status for quality wines produced in the heart of the Prosecco region; and a sub-zone of wine made in the pre-eminent Cartizze hills is now labelled Superiore di Cartizze. The wine may be sparkling (*spumante*) or semi-sparkling (*frizzante*). To prevent any other prosecco producers from marketing inferior sparkling wines, now all prosecco sparkling wine must at least adhere to DOC quality specifications. If wines outside this region are produced with the prosecco grape, they cannot even be termed prosecco. The same grapes outside the

Prosecco DOC must be called *glera*, which is the old dialect name for prosecco.

Italian wine consumers tend to be loyal to their own regions, but over the past decade or so Italians everywhere have begun to order prosecco as an aperitif anytime, anywhere. They're doing the same in the US, which is prosecco's top export market. Other sparkling wine regions in Italy have not made as big an impact with their exports – yet. Piedmont's Brachetto d'Aqui is one of the few very good-quality red sparkling wines exported regularly to the US, where it has a small but growing following.

In the United States, many middle-aged and older people who otherwise drink wine actually seem to be afraid of champagne, firmly believing it must be reserved for one or two special occasions in their lives – perhaps having been initially intimidated by champagne's air of European sophistication (not to mention price). Fortunately, this is beginning to change in younger demographics, with the widespread availability of better-quality sparkling wines at a variety of prices, from a variety of sources. In 2008 more than 50 per cent of the sparkling wine drunk by Americans was from California, 8.6 per cent was from other states and under 40 per cent was from other countries. One California sparkling wine is actively challenging the top French champagne houses: over the past several years Schramsberg has staged blind tastings of its wines along with fine champagnes, for wine professionals. Invariably the new top Schramsberg sparkling wines compare extremely favourably with their French counterparts, and are sometimes judged to be higher quality than champagnes at similar or even higher price levels.

Australians started out with a keen enjoyment of their native sparkling shiraz. This sparkler has evolved, in many instances, into a somewhat finer wine. For serious (traditional method) sparkling wine, Australia's first major sparkling winery Seppelt is still one of the major producers, along with Brian Croser and a number of others in the cooler wine regions of Victoria – especially the Yarra Valley – and Tasmania. Several French champagne houses that established wineries or winery partnerships in these areas are still in business: Moët et Chandon (Green Point), Bollinger (a silent partner in Croser's original winery Petaluma) and Roederer (now Jansz).

Spain's cava has been king domestically, and its popularity has been building outside the country for a good thirty years. In areas of the United States where Brazilian émigrés have congregated, some Brazilian sparkling wines have begun to penetrate the market. Most are sweet, often made by large cooperatives, but a few producers of modern, dryer sparkling wines are beginning to make themselves known both domestically and as exports. In Argentina, Champagne-based wineries with local outposts such as Bodega Mumm and Bodegas Chandon now make a significant proportion of the quality sparkling wine for domestic consumption. In South Africa, though fans have access to champagne, domestic winemakers are becoming more interested in sparkling wine production; today the Cap Classique Producers Association has 55 members.

7
Scandale! Expanding Champagne Around the World

By the end of the twentieth century European sparkling wine producers from France and Spain had stakes in wineries on three other continents: North America, South America and Australia. Their wines were made with care in the traditional method, and they were successful, selling at prices that ranged up to those of mid-level champagnes. Demand was still increasing and it was clear that the champagne houses needed even more land for vineyards. In 2003 the people of Champagne began a debate about changing the revered boundaries of Champagne's vineyards. Officially delimited in 1927, the borders have changed slightly over time, most recently in 1992 when Fontaine-sur-Aÿ took its case to the French high court – and won. As of 2009, another forty communities (*communes*) have been added to the delimited zone for vineyards growing grapes for champagne – but a further 100 petitioning communities did not make the cut. In the years before this, there was a lot of jockeying for position. Champagne houses were assumed to have the upper hand because they would have the financial resources to purchase vineyards in the suddenly expensive, newly included communities – if the land-owners wanted to sell. Alternatively, the land-owners who could afford (or borrow enough) to produce their own

Unmask the truth...

AMERICAN CHAMPAGNE

★

Extra Dry

No more cover-ups.

It's not just subprime mortgages and derivative insurance that bury honesty in legal mumbo jumbo. A legal loophole allows some U.S. wines to masquerade as something they're not.

There are many fine sparkling wines, but only those from **Champagne** can use that region's name. Names of American wine regions like Napa Valley and Willamette are also misused.

Consumer groups agree: deceptive wine labeling must stop. Tell Congress to protect consumers. Sign the petition at **www.champagne.us**.

Champagne *only* comes from Champagne, France.

CHAMPAGNE BUREAU

Producers of French champagne have secured agreements from many other wine regions not to use the word 'champagne' on their sparkling wine labels. They have also launched a campaign for public awareness of the issue with advertisements like this one.

champagne would be in much better positions. However, in order to create new vineyards, until 2018 everyone has to get permission to plant from the European Union (EU) – and the current EU trend is to take out vineyards because of over-production of wine, especially in France. It's worth noting that extending the Champagne region does not necessarily dilute the classification; rather, it may put established growers as well as producers on notice that they will be under more scrutiny to improve their vineyards and make better wines. The new vineyards, after all, are adjacent to the 1927 bound-aries, and everyone knows that politics plays a certain part in creating borders.

Continuing to look for vineyard lands, many of the cham-pagne houses have covertly had their eyes on England for the past few years, with some, like Roederer, openly exploring possibilities. Climate change has apparently increased yields in Champagne and has allowed its neighbour across the Channel to have vineyards where grapes now ripen enough during the growing season to make good sparkling wines. The newest contender with vineyards in Hampshire is Christian Seely, head of the wine division of France's AXA corporation, which is already an investor in top vineyards and wineries in several countries. Also in 2009, British supermarket chain Waitrose planted vineyards in Hampshire, to produce its own sparkling wine. In the same year, British wine authority Steven Spurrier and his wife planted vines for sparkling wine production on their property in Dorset. Hotel and retail magnate Richard Balfour-Lynn bought vineyards as early as 2002 and now pro-duces sparkling wine in Kent.

English sparkling wines are winning prizes. Ridgeview's Merret Bloomsbury 2002 received the Best Sparkling Wine award at the 2005 International Wine and Spirit Competition in London, against wines from Australia, California and Italy, among others. Ridgeview is one of the top English sparkling wine producers, others being Camel Valley, Chapel Down, Denbies, Bolney Wine Estate and Nyetimber. With vineyards 150 miles north of the latitude of the city of Épernay in Champagne, these producers are on the edge of viability for champagne grapes – just as the vineyards of Champagne were until the recent climate change, many people believe. Most English sparkling wine makers grow the traditional champagne grapes and vinify them in the traditional manner, though a few also make wines with hybrid grapes created for northern climates.

With such competition right on their doorstep – let alone in wine regions all over the world – how can the sparkling wine producers of Champagne continue to protect their brand? In part, with the backing of the European Union. From 1994 on, winemakers in the EU have not been allowed to use the word 'champagne' on their labels. They have even changed the terminology for sparkling wine production from the 'champagne method' (*méthode champenoise*) to the 'traditional method'. Some sparkling wine companies in the United States – and elsewhere – are resisting this. One result is the campaign by the Office of Champagne, USA, running in food magazines and other upscale publications, with a variety of images and taglines to make their point. One tactic questions 'Monterey Jack from Alaska? Washington Apples from Nevada?' Another campaign has a photo of an elegant lady's mask for a costume ball, and reads: 'Masquerading as Champagne . . . might be legal but it isn't fair.' Bit by bit, winemakers in many regions have agreed with the Champagne producers not to use the word 'champagne' on their labels – Napa, California winemakers as late as 2005.

8

Drinking Today:
What, Where and How

Today trends in sparkling wine and champagne have led to increased availability of rosé sparkling wines and champagnes; increased production of the driest categories of champagne; sparkling wines exported by more wine regions worldwide; organic sparkling wine and champagne; brightly coloured bottles and labels, some in individual serving sizes (187.5 ml); and easier-opening closures (like Maestro®, which has a handle that lifts up and uncorks with a pop, and Zork®, a reclosable, recyclable, cork-shaped plastic top that also promises a popping sound when released).

Two of these trends, drier and rosé sparkling wines, could both be the result of recent climate change allowing the grapes to ripen more fully and the wines to carry more full fruit flavours and aromas than in the past. Rosé wines have become very popular as their quality has improved (and sweetness has abated). Australians have been drinking light red sparkling shiraz as a casual and holiday wine for many years now, and perhaps this has also had an effect on global attitudes.

On a sparkling wine label, the word 'champagne' is now a quality guarantee only if it is made in the Champagne region of France. Sparkling wines from nearby Alsace and the rest of France are developing followings. Cava from Spain is an

The new 'Maestro' closure, tested at Champagne Duval-Leroy, makes it easier to open champagne and sparkling wine bottles.

The new Zork SPK closure for champagne and sparkling wine also functions as a resealable top for opened bottles.

Sparkling wine vineyards on the slopes surround tiny, picturesque villages in Alsace.

excellent beverage that has been leading exports in price. In the US, sparkling wines from California lead the way, followed distantly by other states including Washington, Oregon, New York, New Mexico and Massachusetts. Despite the recession, Italy's prosecco exports rose 8 per cent in 2008. Prosecco has been disdained by the British – especially the British wine press – until recent price and quality improvements have also led to sales doubling there.

Champagne still reigns throughout the world in terms of price and prestige. Worldwide shipments of champagne totalled 338,707,192 bottles in 2007 and this was down only about five per cent during the economic downturn of 2008. Nearly 44 per cent of champagne is exported.

Since champagne remains the 'gold standard' of sparkling wine, it's useful to understand what's in a bottle before

purchasing it. Essentially, champagne is made with three grapes – one white and two red: chardonnay, pinot noir and pinot meunier. In actuality, nine named grapes can go into champagne: chardonnay, pinot noir, pinot meunier, pinot blanc, arbanne, petit meslier, pinot gris (also called *fromenteau* in Champagne), pinot de juillet and pinot rosé. Some of these grapes are pinot variations and may not be strictly defined as different grapes. According to champagne expert Peter Liem, champagne can legally be made from grapes in the pinot family – including chardonnay, which was formerly referred to as 'pinot chardonnay' – as well as the arbanne and petit meslier grapes. Of the grapes in Champagne 98 per cent are chardonnay, pinot noir and pinot meunier, most often blended together in proprietary styles by different champagne houses. Blanc de blancs is made only with chardonnay grapes; blanc de noirs is made only with red grapes. Pinot noir is generally responsible for the colour in rosé champagnes. Pinot meunier

Thousands of bottles of champagne ageing underground in the chalk cellars of the Champagne region.

has traditionally appeared in champagne blends in very small amounts, though recently some grower-producers have begun making champagnes that feature this grape. The terms blanc de blancs and blanc de noirs are also used in other regions to reflect sparkling wines made with only white grapes and only red grapes.

A finished champagne labelled NV (non-vintage) can only be released for sale fifteen months after harvest, at the earliest. Most are aged longer, eighteen months, and sometimes thirty or more for a special blend. Instead of NV, some producers are starting to use the term MV (multi-vintage) because it sounds more positive. The top blends of each champagne house are known as the *têtes de cuvée*, also called *prestige cuvées*. For a champagne to be labelled 'vintage', 100 per cent of the grapes must come from that year's harvest, and the year of harvest is printed on the label.

A 'Grande Marque' is a champagne house that produces a great quality or volume of champagne. Each usually produces

Blending wines for champagne. A producer may work with a dozen or more wines from different vineyards.

a variety of champagnes from non-vintage to proprietarily named blends, to vintage champagnes – and a variety of styles from brut to extra dry – some of which are rosés. Most champagne houses do not own their own vineyards. They buy grapes from designated vineyards. On the labels, their champagnes may be marked NM, for Négociant-Manipulant, if they buy grapes from growers to make their champagne. RM means Récoltant-Manipulant: a grower who makes champagne mainly with his own grapes. Over the past twenty years a new cluster of small grower-producers has appeared in the Champagne region. These are people who have their own vineyards, and/or have access to grapes approved for making champagne. They have built small production facilities, sometimes literally in their basements, where they produce hundreds of bottles per year, often tunnelling further under their property for storage space. These are legal and legitimate champagnes. As a group, the wines have shown dramatic improvement in both consistency of quality and complexity of taste. The

A proud range of champagnes from grower-producer Moussé Fils.

winemakers also have the freedom to create their own blending strategies, which can evolve from harvest to harvest, unlike the large champagne houses whose identity lies in their reliable house styles.

In Champagne, sparkling wine is categorized by the amount of pressure in the bottle. Early champagnes were limited by technology to only a few atmospheres of pressure. Now, sparkling wine under 2.5 atmospheres is called *perlant*. *Pétillant* means the sparkling wine in the bottle is between 2.5 and 3.5 atmospheres. *Crémant*, in Champagne, generally refers to wines around 3.6 atmospheres, although (as mentioned earlier) other regions and countries may call any sparkling wine 'crémant'. Though champagnes are allowed to be anywhere above 3.5 atmospheres, they are generally 5 to 6 atmospheres. This is also referred to as *mousseux* or *grand mousseux* in France, *espumante* in Portugal, *espumoso* in Spain, *spumante* in Italy, and *sparkling wine* in English-speaking countries.

Photograph of microscopic bubble formations by expert champagne researcher and photographer Gérard Liger-Belair.

At the Laurent-Perrier champagne house, this fountain's motto understandably reads 'Never Drink Water'.

The smaller the bubbles, the better the champagne – myth or reality? Regularity and persistence of bubbles are important in sparkling wine and champagne. Champagne researcher Gérard Liger-Belair has recently discovered that champagne bubbles contain up to thirty times more aromas and flavours than the liquid. Continuous streams of fine bubbles act as a flavour delivery system in the mouth, too. Before this discovery, champagne makers and enthusiasts had believed that the smaller and more regular streams of bubbles were best, but they didn't have the science to back up their impressions. Liger-Belair estimates that up to 11 million bubbles can escape from one flute of champagne, which contains about a tenth of a litre of wine.

The style of a champagne or sparkling wine is defined by a measure called residual sugar; sparkling wine grapes are prized for acidity, which must be perfectly counterbalanced with a measured (often imperceptible) amount of sweetness. With climate changes in recent years, the grapes in Champagne's vineyards have achieved more ripe flavours and aromas than in the past. Many New World vineyards receive more heat and sun than in Champagne, so their grapes are riper when harvested. The positive results of this are felt most in the two driest styles of wine: brut nature and extra brut. Brut nature has no dosage at all: it is a 'natural' sparkling wine, and can only be made in the ripest vintages. Extra brut is almost as 'natural' with as little dosage as possible added – just enough to fully balance the acidity in the grapes. The champagne houses Laurent-Perrier and Piper-Heidsieck have made specialities of these styles which they call 'ultra brut' and 'brut sauvage' wines.

Style definitions for champagne are similar to prosecco and other quality sparkling wines. Rosé champagnes and sparkling wines can be made in any style; the fashion today is for

Crates of large format bottles await labelling at Pol Roger. The ageing cellars are so humid that the labels and foil capsules must be added just before the champagnes are shipped out.

brut rosé. Residual sugar is measured in grams per litre (g/l). Very small changes in the amount of sugar affect the perception of fruitiness and other flavours – not only of sweetness on the tongue. Brut nature is defined as carrying less than 3 g/l (also known as brut sauvage, brut non-dosé, brut zéro and zéro dosage). Extra brut or ultra brut has less than 6 g/l, brut has less than 15 g/l, extra dry has 12–20 g/l, sec or dry has 17–35 g/l, demi sec has 35–50g/l. Doux or sweet champagne has over 50 g/l and is unfortunately nearly extinct in the twenty-first century.

In Champagne, large bottles were named after historic and biblical figures that represented greatness to the champagne producers who selected them at the end of the nineteenth century. Large-format bottles – larger than a single bottle of 750 ml – will age progressively more slowly, so the champagne's producer should be consulted about when to open the larger bottles. It's best to drink the smaller sizes (quarter and half bottles) as soon as possible after purchase.

Bottle sizes

Quart/Quarter bottle = 187.5–200 ml (single serving, often used by airlines)

Demi/half bottle = 375 ml (also called a 'split' in the US)

Bottle = 750 ml

Magnum = 1.5 litres or 2 bottles

Jeroboam = 3 litres (4 bottles)

Rehoboam = 4.5 litres (6 bottles)

Methuselah = 6 litres (8 bottles)

Salamanazar = 9 litres (12 bottles)

Balthazar = 12 litres (16 bottles)

Nebuchadnezzar = 15 litres (20 bottles)

Champagne Rules:
Buying, Storing, Serving

In the French region of Champagne, people drink champagne with dinner, treating it as if it were their local wine – which, of course, it is. Elsewhere in the world a range of attitudes towards sparkling wines prevail, from 'weddings only' to sipping a glass of cava as a daily aperitif.

Champagne is not better or worse than 'sparkling wine' because champagne is simply sparkling wine from the Champagne region of France. In some instances, there are better sparkling wines than champagnes at the same price. With the advantage of experience and marketing, the very top quality and very top price sparkling wines tend to come from Champagne, where the prestige of the house (producer) also contributes.

It used to be that the more expensive the champagne, the better the quality. Today, this general guideline is somewhat complicated by the plethora of sparkling wines being produced worldwide. However, most sparkling wines cannot yet command the prices of the top champagnes. At the highest end, we find special *cuvées* (blends) released by the top champagne houses. Some are commemorative, celebrating special events such as a royal wedding, the turn of the century or a special vintage in Champagne. A bottle costs several hundred dollars (£150 plus) at least.

The ultra-modern tasting room at Champagne Salon, a prestige producer in Le Mesnil-sur-Oger in the Champagne region of France.

A champagne house such as Krug creates exclusive blends from small plots in select vineyards, and has achieved a high level of fame and pricing based on reputation. Salon, equally prestigious, produces champagne only from the chardonnay grown in its own enclosed vineyard and the nearby vineyard parcels chosen by the founder of the house ninety years ago. Two other well-known champagne houses produce the high-end proprietarily named champagnes most famous around the world: Roederer's Cristal and Moët et Chandon's Dom Pérignon.

Most houses produce champagnes for special occasions in a range of quality and pricing, with reserve, rosé and other special *cuvées* starting around $100 (£50 plus); there is occasional discounting, especially around the holidays.

A good place to begin experiencing fine French champagnes is with non-vintage bottles that begin in the $40–50

(£25–30 in the UK) range. Note that very few non-champagne sparkling wines are priced over $50 (£30). From this price range up, choosing a champagne tends to be a matter of personal preference, honed by tasting and personal recommendations.

A few top champagne houses and cava producers have wineries in the United States where they produce sparkling wines at prices in the $30–50 (£15–30 in the UK) range. The best sparkling wines from California's Napa and Sonoma are in this price range, and of equally fine quality, including Iron Horse, J and Schramsberg. The same group also have very good sparkling wines in the next lowest price category, around $20–30 (£10–15) in the US. British shops tend to stock more Australian, European and their own English sparkling wines in the £15–20 ($30–40) price range. They may also offer champagnes of this quality privately labelled with the shop's names. Popular English sparkling wine producers include Bolney, Camel Valley, Chapel Down, Denbies, Nyetimber and Ridgeview.

French crémant sparkling wines from Alsace have dominated the next price range (beginning around $20 or £10 in the UK) in the US, with Burgundy, the Loire and others now catching up. Moving down a notch in price, supermarket brand champagnes and sparkling wines are readily available in Britain, and their quality can be quite good, while in the US, reasonably priced, better-quality sparkling wines – $20 (£10), plus or minus – are often imported from Spain and Italy and include very good cavas and proseccos.

If the goal is to procure just any sparkling wine the prices begin a lot lower, under $10 in the US and under £5 in the UK. However, in the UK holiday discounts on sparkling wines are tremendous and even French champagnes can be found in the large supermarkets for extremely low prices at the end of the year. It's rare that a good sparkling wine is found under $10 in the US; Freixenet's cavas are one great exception, when discounted slightly.

Often, multiple bottles of the lowest-end wines are purchased for an event, and it is important to taste one bottle before buying many. In the US, several of the oldest producers, such as Korbel, Inglenook and Great Western, fall into this category; note that they may put the word 'champagne' on their labels for a variety of reasons. Several other countries, especially Australia, Italy and France, also contribute sparkling wines to the lowest price point level in the US and UK, though they tend not to use 'champagne' on their labels. Purchases at this level of sparkling wine tend to be price-driven.

In Hollywood, Moët et Chandon's 'White Star' – recently renamed 'Imperial' – became popular in the latter part of the twentieth century as an 'everyday champagne', with Mumm's Cordon Rouge a close second; this is echoed in many parts of America where the preference is for a light and lively style with a touch of fruit in the flavours and aromas. In Britain, the taste runs more to toasty champagnes like the long-imported Bollinger and Billecart-Salmon. Elsewhere around the world, people's selection tends to depend on local availability. For extra special occasions – where more money is being spent – many will choose champagnes such as Perrier-Jouet's Fleur de Champagne, Veuve Clicquot's La Grande Dame and Taittinger's Comte de Champagne. Champagnes Krug and Salon are reserved for those who are enthralled by the taste of one or other of these particular champagnes – and can afford them. One champagne, Dom Pérignon, translates as *the* symbol of fine champagne worldwide.

Non-vintage champagnes and sparkling wines do not need to be aged once purchased. Generally, it's best to consume these wines within one to two years after they are released. This usually means within one or two years after you buy it, as long as your wine shop is good about turning over their stock. If you're not sure how long a bottle has been languishing on the shelf – either yours or the shop's – open it sooner rather than later. Countless people mistakenly spend decades guarding a bottle of non-vintage sparkling wine received for their birthday, wedding or anniversary, only to find it flat and faded when finally opened.

Quality sparkling wines need the same cool and humid storage conditions as other wines, with one exception: they can be stored upright. The cork does not need to be kept moistened for years because most champagnes will not be stored for years, and because the pressure in the bottle keeps the air inside humidified. Also, the cork on a bottle of sparkling wine is more tightly compressed and it is wired in place, so it is less likely to shrink or become loosened. Ideal storage has a humidity level of 60 per cent and a temperature of 50–55°F (10–12°C). A regular (food) refrigerator is fine for short periods of time; however, it is a little more drying and a little colder than optimal wine storage conditions. As with still wines, champagnes do best in constant conditions; variations in temperature can be most harmful. Keeping sparkling wines cool is imperative to minimize the risk of corks shooting off or bottles bursting because they contain wine under pressure.

With vintage champagne it's important to remember that just because a bottle has a vintage date on it, this does not mean it should be stored for more than the usual year or two. Champagne houses release their wines when they are ready to be consumed. (One rare exception to this rule of early consumption might be vintage champagne that has been purchased from a specialist and is part of a collection. Collectors tend to have perfect storage spaces and top advisors for this purpose.)

When you are ready to drink champagne and sparkling wine, it's important that the bottles be chilled. Some people plunge them into ice baths or into the freezer, which, though it may be all right for the lesser wines, is not the best way to treat a fine wine. Instead, put it into a refrigerator, where it will chill down gradually over the course of four to six hours. Champagne stored in a kitchen refrigerator is a bit too cold to drink; it should be taken out about twenty minutes before serving. Serve sparkling wine at 45–50°F (8–10°C).

To open a bottle of champagne, place the bottle on a flat surface. Have a champagne glass nearby, and a cloth at hand in case the bottle is slippery. Untwist the wire cage (*muselet*) that holds the cork while keeping a thumb on top of the cork in case it starts to come out of the bottle. The cork should not shoot out if the sparkling wine is nicely chilled. Point the top of the bottle away from people and valuable possessions, keeping it upright or at a slight angle. Six twists of the wire will generally free the cage from the cork. Hold the

cork in place on the bottle with one hand, and slowly rotate the bottle with the other hand, gently easing the cork out. The cork should exit the bottle with a gentle sigh, not a pop. The only time you want a bottle to pop is if you have shaken it up to foam over someone during a sports victory.

Sabrage is the art of slashing off the top of a champagne bottle with a sabre or sword. Supposedly, soldiers in Napoleon's army began the practice as they were riding through Champagne on a military campaign, with no time to spare. Today, *sabrage* (also called 'sabring') is performed at public events, often with a special 'champagne sword' which looks like a small, straight scimitar. Sometimes the sabred champagne is used to start a champagne fountain with a pyramid of glasses for a showy opening to a special event. Sabred champagne is considered completely safe to drink because when the top of the bottle is sliced off, some of the champagne shoots out, carrying the bottle top and any pieces of glass with it. Little champagne is lost when the bottle is held

Step 1. Unwrap and remove the foil covering the cork and wire cage on top of the bottle.

Step 2. Holding the cork in place with one hand, turn the bottle until the cork begins to loosen in the neck of the bottle.

Step 3. Ease the cork out of the bottle. You will hear a gentle sigh – not a loud pop – when this is done properly.

Step 4. Pour the sparkling wine gently, and only half-fill the glass. This puts the surface of the liquid at the widest part of the glass, optimal for relishing the wine's aromas.

When the correct amount of champagne is poured, it remains cool and sparkly, and a pleasure to sip, until the glass is finished.

at the correct angle during sabring. Of course, *sabrage* is only performed by experts.

For glassware, on the table, a coupe wineglass looks pretty but it is only really functional if there is someone at your shoulder pouring in chilled champagne a few mouthfuls at a time, just as you are ready to sip from the glass. For the rest of us, the right type of glass is a flute or a smallish white wine glass. The champagne flute is a definite improvement over the flat coupe. It has an elegant stem which you can hold without warming the liquid in the glass with the body heat in your fingers. It's tall and clear, so you can appreciate the lines of fine bubbles snaking their elegant ways to the top of the liquid. The diameter of the flute's top is slightly smaller than the bowl to hold in the aroma of the sparkling wine. The same is true of a white wine glass: a small, tulip-shaped glass with a stem, with an even larger diameter than its rim, allowing more of the pleasant aromas to collect in the top of the glass.

Poured correctly, a sparkling wine fills half of the glass. In a flute or tulip-shaped glass, this puts the surface of the wine in the largest part of the bowl. With a larger surface, more bubbles are popping and delivering their aromas to your nose, even before you sip the wine. When you incline your head over the top of the glass, you experience not only the pleasant light hissing of the bubbles popping on the liquid's surface, you gain a generous hint of the flavours of the sparkling wine you're about to imbibe. Sometimes the quality, quantity and persistence of bubbles are affected by invisible residue in the glass; if this occurs it's best to ask for a different glass, and/or wipe the glass out with a cloth; do not rinse with water, which could have left the residue in the first place.

In addition to the proper glassware there is really nothing else needed to complete the enjoyment of a sparkling wine. No special openers or decanters. As champagne tends to be consumed once a bottle is opened, there's rarely a need for a stopper. Champagne stoppers are inexpensive and can be useful occasionally. Truthfully, a small teaspoon (dessertspoon) works, too; insert the spoon into the neck of a bottle of unfinished sparkling wine, store it in a refrigerator, and it will hold its fizz for a good twenty-four hours – long enough to enjoy with brunch the day after.

What to Have with your Champagne and Sparkling Wine

Often, brut sparkling wine is best served as an aperitif, on its own, without food. Some can also be paired with smoky tastes, caviar being the classic example. Oysters and other seafood may be served with a more delicate champagne or sparkling wine. If the wine is full-bodied, it can be drunk throughout a light meal. With these wines, foie gras is a classic first course in the region of Champagne.

Rosé and other pinot noir based champagnes are heartier, and will carry through the fish or poultry courses of a meal.

Extra dry sparkling wines have a wide range of accompaniment possibilities, from light, savoury hors d'oeuvres to light dishes for a first course such as pasta, risotto and fish.

Extra dry and sweet sparkling wines – as well as many rosés – are also lovely with dried fruits like figs and dates. Nuts such as walnuts, chestnuts and almonds also make good accompaniments, and can be offered plain, roasted, lightly salted or smoked.

The sweetest sparkling wines can be served with fruitcakes, pound cakes and similarly plain cakes and cookies. Some fresh fruits with a lot of sugar and acidity are good garnishes, especially raspberries and strawberries, but only if they are very ripe.

With sparkling wines, it's best to stay away from dairy-based foods like soft cheeses and milk chocolate. The fats in these will coat the mouth and cancel out the texture and flavours of the delicate sparkling wine. Though with a rosé, it's OK to very occasionally try a bite of very dark chocolate.

Classic Cocktail Recipes for Champagne and Sparkling Wine

Bellini

Pour 2 ounces (60 ml) of chilled fresh, white peach puree into a champagne flute. Add 4 ounces (120 ml) of prosecco. Stir lightly.

Black Velvet

Fill a beer mug halfway with Guinness, then carefully add an equal amount of chilled sparkling wine or champagne.

Buck's Fizz

Mix 3 ounces (90 ml) of chilled orange juice and ¼ an ounce (7.5 ml) of gin in a champagne flute. Add 3 ounces (90 ml) of chilled champagne and stir lightly. Garnish with half a slice of orange.

Champagne Bowler

Put 3 coarsely chopped strawberries and ½ an ounce (15 ml) of simple syrup (sugar syrup) into a cocktail shaker. Add ice cubes, ½ an ounce (15 ml) of cognac and 1 ounce (30 ml) of chilled white wine. Shake, then strain into a wine glass. Add 3 ounces (90 ml) of chilled champagne.

Champagne Cocktail

Place 1 cube or lump of sugar in the bottom of a champagne flute. Pour several drops of bitters onto the sugar. Slowly pour 4 ounces (120 ml) of chilled champagne down the side of the glass. Garnish with a twist of lemon peel.

Death in the Afternoon

Pour 1 ounce (30 ml) of absinthe into the bottom of a champagne flute. Add chilled champagne or sparkling wine until the liquid turns cloudy.

French 75

In a cocktail shaker with ice, pour 1 ounce (30 ml) of gin, ½ an ounce (15 ml) of simple syrup (sugar syrup) and ½ an ounce (15 ml) of fresh lemon juice. Shake well and strain into a flute or Collins glass. Top with 3 ounces (90 ml) of chilled champagne. Garnish with a thin lemon slice or spiral.

Kir Royale

Pour 4 ounces (120 ml) of chilled champagne into a champagne flute. Slowly pour in ½ an ounce (15 ml) of crème de cassis down the edge of the glass, creating a layered effect of champagne over cassis.

Mimosa

Pour 3 ounces (90 ml) of chilled orange juice into a champagne flute. Add three ounces of chilled champagne. Stir lightly. Garnish with orange or mint.

Ritz Fizz

Pour ½ a teaspoon of simple syrup (sugar syrup) into the bottom of a champagne flute. Add ¼ of a teaspoon each of Diasronno and Curaçao and mix. Add 4 ounces (120 ml) of chilled champagne.

Valencia

Pour 2 ounces (60 ml) of apricot brandy, 1 ounce (30 ml) of orange juice and 4 drops of bitters into a shaker with ice and stir well. Strain into a flute and add 4 ounces (120 ml) of chilled, extra dry cava or other sparkling wine.

Veneziana Spritz

Pour 1 ounce (30 ml) of Aperol into a white wine glass. Add 2 ounces (60 ml) of chilled prosecco and 2 ounces (60 ml) of chilled sparkling mineral water or club soda. Stir lightly.

Select Bibliography

Anderson, Burton, *Franciacorta: Italy's Sanctuary of Sparkling Wine* (Milan, 2002)

Crestin-Billet, Frédérique, *Veuve Cliquot: La Grande Dame de la Champagne* (Grenoble, 1992), trans. Carol Fahy

Gately, Iain, *Drink: A Cultural History of Alcohol* (New York, 2008)

Glatre, Eric, *Champagne Guide* (New York, 1999)

——, *Champagne: Pleasure Shared* (Paris, 2000)

——, *Chronique des Vins de Champagne* (Chassigny, 2001)

Gronow, Jukka, *Caviar with Champagne: Common Luxury and the Ideals of the Good Life in Stalin's Russia* (Oxford, 2003)

Guy, K. M., *When Champagne Became French* (Baltimore, MD, 2003)

Johnson, Hugh, *The Story of Wine: New Illustrated Edition* (London, 2002)

——, and Jancis Robinson, *The World Atlas of Wine*, 5th edn (London, 2001)

Liger-Belair, Gérard, *Uncorked: The Science of Champagne* (Princeton, NJ, 2004)

Lukacs, Paul, *American Vintage: The Rise of American Wine* (Boston, MA, 2000)

McCarthy, Ed, *Champagne for Dummies* (Foster City, CA, 1999)

Simon, Andre L., *The History of Champagne* (London, 1971)

Stevenson, Tom, *World Encyclopedia of Champagne and Sparkling Wine* (San Francisco, CA, 2003)

Sutcliffe, Serena, *Champagne: The History and Character of the World's Most Celebrated Wine* (New York, 1988)

Websites and Associations

Austrian Wine
www.austrian.wine.co.at/eindex.html

California Wine Institute
www.wineinstitute.org

Cap Classique Producers Association, South Africa
www.capclassique.co.za

Champagne Information Bureau, UK
www.champagne-civc.co.uk

Conegliano Valdobbiadene Prosecco Superiore, Italy
www.prosecco.it

Foods and Wines of Italy, Italian Trade Commission
www.italianmade.com

Office of Champagne, USA
www.champagne.us

Union of Champagne Houses, France
http://maisons-champagne.com

Wine Australia
www.wineaustralia.com/australia

Wines from Spain
www.winesfromspain.com

Wines of Germay
www.germanwineusa.com
www.winesofgermany.co.uk

Acknowledgements

Countless people helped me to understand this elegant beverage, from vine to bottle. Thank you to: the Office of Champagne, Mark Destito, Jean Card; Le Comité Interprofessionnel du Vin de Champagne (CIVC), Philippe Wibrotte, Chrystelle Perraud, Brigitte Batonnet; l'Office de Tourisme de Reims; Moët-Hennessy, Jeff Pogash, Corinne Perez; Champagne Houses Duval-Leroy, Henri Abelé, Henriet-Bazin, Jacquesson, Moussé, Pol Roger, Pommery-Vranken, Roger Coulon, Ruinart, Salon et Delamotte and Veuve Clicquot; Jean-Louis Carbonnier; Eric Glâtre; Peter Liem; Maxime Toubart; Groupe des Jeunes Vignerons de Champagne; Wilson Daniels, Lori Narlock, Lisa Mattson; English Wine Producers, Julia Trustram Eve; WineAustralia; Napa Valley Vintners, Sonoma Valley Vintners & Growers Alliance, Gloria Ferrer, J, Schramsberg; Bureau Interprofessionnel des Vins de Bourgogne, Cécile Mathiaud; Consorzio Tutela Prosecco di Conegliano Valdobbiadene, Michèle Shah, Silvia Baratta, Adami, Astoria, Bellussi, Bepin de Eto, Bisol, Bortolomiol, Col Vetoraz, Drusian, Mionetto, Tenuta di Collalto, Valdo Spumanti and Zardetto; Jill and Dale DeGroff, A. J. Rathbun; Bisso Atanassov; Branko Gerovac, Ken Simonson and Jan Solomon – and everyone who raised a glass of champagne or sparkling wine with me!

Photo Acknowledgements

The author and the publishers wish to express their thanks to the below sources of illustrative material and/or permission to reproduce it.

Roger Archey: p. 63; Archives départementales – Conseil Général de l'Aube: p. 72; BIVB/ J. Gesvres: p. 76; Bollinger Private Collection: p. 75; Branko Gerovac: pp. 64, 106, 108, 109, 112; courtesy of Champagne Ayala: p. 44; Champagne Bureau: p. 97; Collection CIVIC: pp. 13 (Visuel Impact), 14 (Alain Cornu), 18 (Fulvio Roiter), 22 (Frederick Hadengue), 24 (Claude & Françoise Huyghens Danrigal), 27 (Hubert de Sanatana), 28 (Visuel Impact), 29 (John Hodder), 35 (Berengo Gardin), 36 (DIVERS), 46 top and bottom (Claude & Françoise Huyghens Danrigal), 57 (John Hodder), 61, 62 (Kumasegawa), 87 (John Hodder), 104 (Berengo Gardin), 105 (Visuel Impact), 116, 117, 118 (Kumasegawa), 119 (Photo Fabrice Leseigneur); courtesy Conegliano Valdobbiadene Prosecco Superiore Consortium: p. 82; Conseil Interprofessionnel des Vins du Languedoc: p. 17; Becky Sue Epstein: p. 37; Johann Fitz – Weingut Fitz-Ritter & Sektkellerei Fitz KG: p. 55; courtesy of Freixenet: pp. 83, 84; Istockphoto: p. 6 (Gradisca); Maestro®, Zork®: p. 101; Michel Jolyot: p. 23; Laurent-Perrier: p. 108; Gérard Liger-Belair: p. 107; Jeff Pogash: p. 21; Fabrice Rambert: p. 10; courtesy of Simonnet-Febvre: p. 77; Tom Sullam Photography: p. 8; Terry Theise: p. 59; University of California, San Diego: p. 47; VinsAlsace.com: pp. 102 (F. Zvardon), 103 (F. Zvardon).

Index

italic numbers refer to illustrations; **bold** to recipes